Change Your Handwriting,

Change Your Life

Change Your Handwriting, Change Your Life

Vimala Rodgers

Celestial Arts
Berkeley, California

Change Your Handwriting, Change Your Life

Cover design by Fifth Street Design

Text design by Victor Ichioka

Library of Congress Cataloging-in-Publication Data

Rodgers, Vimala,
    Change your handwriting, change your life / Vimala Rodgers.
        p.   cm.
    ISBN 0-89087-693-2
        1. Graphology.   I. Title
BF901.R63   1993   93-6843
155.2'82—dc20

2 3 4 5 6 7 8 / 99 98 97 96 95

I dedicate this book

to those teachers who have had

the most profound impact on my life,

each uniquely: Ram Dass;

my very best friend,

Paramhansa Yogananda;

and my children, Jean-Marie, Stephanie,

Siobhan, Matthew John, Marcus Aurelius,

Amanda, Sara, & Luke.

ACKNOWLEDGMENT

Sincere acknowledgments to my dear and trusted friends Mike Genzmer, Ann McLaughlin, Jo Ann Deck, and Marcy Calhoun. Without the relentless encouragement of Mike and Ann, this book would not have been written. Without Jo Ann's gentle wisdom, support, and humorous heart touches, it would not have been published. Without Marcy's unfailing guidance and love, I would not be here today.

TABLE OF CONTENTS

Who is Vimala?

Once people hear of my profession, the first question I am asked is, "What is graphotherapy?" The next question is, "What is your background?" or "Where did you receive your training?" I respond with this story.

When I was two years old, the milkman made deliveries in his truck and left our milk in glass bottles on the doorstep. My mother would leave empty bottles on the back porch, and every few days the milkman would come and replace them with full ones. Whenever she wanted something extra, like cottage cheese or butter, she would write a list on a small piece of paper and slip it into the neck of an empty bottle. When the milkman came he would read the list, go out to his truck, and bring back what she had ordered.

I remember that my mother and the milkman were often unpleasant with one another. After the milk delivery, she would often grumble that he had not left the additional items she had requested. When she confronted him the next time around, he would say that there had been no note, and my mother (a woman of strong will) would insist that she had left one. Their relationship was an ongoing confrontation.

One day my mother had an especially long list of extra items for the milkman to leave, and rather than busy herself in another part of the house, she stood by the window, peeked from behind the curtains so as not to be seen, and watched him as he made his regular stops in the neighborhood. "I was going to make sure he left all the items I had listed, and if he didn't, I was ready to chase him out to his truck and get them myself!"

She watched him as he finished the delivery at the next-door neighbor's, then sat in his truck momentarily and wrote down his post-delivery notes. "My eyes had him in range, like a camera on close-up, when, suddenly, out of the corner of my eye, I saw movement on the back porch. I leaned over to get a better look and I saw you take the note from the milk bottle and go back into the house. I was livid! Then in a flash I realized, 'Wait a minute. She can't read!' and I raced down the hall."

When my mother found me I was in the back corner of my bedroom closet actively stuffing the note in an old shoe box. When she took the note from me, the shoe box tipped over and out spilled old shopping lists, scribbled notes, hand-addressed envelopes, and old lists she had left for the milkman. Why had I saved them? Although I couldn't read, I "saw" people in handwriting. I had samples from my mom and dad, my favorite aunts and uncles, my godmother, my grandmother, some of my grandmother's friends, and many people I have since forgotten. Having a sample of someone's writing was like having a treasured photograph.

Through the years I read every book I could find on the subject, and by the time I was fourteen or fifteen I was able to distinguish which information was accurate and which was nonsense. I collected handwriting samples from schoolmates, teachers, neighbors, and friends. I ran my own ongoing studies of individual letter formations, margins, or spacings that fascinated me, and reached my own empirical conclusions. I also learned, when I was quite young, that by talking about what I knew about the relationship between handwriting and personality, I was thought to be different, odd, or strange, and that no one played with you if you fit into one of those categories. So, I learned to keep what I knew secret, except for sharing it with a few trusted friends.

I attended college, married, raised a family, and played all the appropriate roles, but I always had handwriting in my back pocket, so to speak. I began to do analyses for friends, and then I gradually expanded my boundaries. Speaking about what I knew came slowly at first, but through the years people began to tell me what a difference my analyses had made in their lives, and I became a little bolder.

When I was asked what my training was, I replied, "I have no formal training." I felt I lost credibility. To counter this, I signed up for a correspondence course in handwriting analysis, just so I could have initials after my name. These were very expensive initials! As the lessons began to arrive, I realized how the information, although accurate, lacked depth. It dealt only with symptoms and labeled them "good" or "bad." The result was that I began to see clearly how much I really *did* know, and I began to value the in-depth approach I had taken throughout the years. As I look back now, I see that obtaining those initials after my name was more important for *me* than for the client.As I became more sure of myself, I dispensed with them altogether. And now, boldly, I have written a book. We spend a lifetime hiding from our own greatness, layering ourselves with concealing attitudes. My purpose in writing *Change Your Handwriting, Change Your Life* is to give you, the reader, a simple, nonthreatening tool with which to peel away those protective layers with reverence and gentleness. As they silently fall away, may you delight in exposing and exploring the "new" you who has been there all along. Tag. You're it!

CHAPTER ONE

One Stroke at a Time

HANDWRITING IS FAR more than just a string of words put together to create a means of communication. To a skilled handwriting analyst, it is a diagram of a person's attitude toward life. To a trained graphotherapist, it is a direct path to long-forgotten hiding places inside each person. Although the hand (or teeth, or toes) holds the pen, it is the brain that causes it to move as it does. When we write, each movement of the pen not only reflects the attitudes we have about our circumstances and ourselves, it also reinforces them. Each time we press the pen to the paper, create a margin, or shape a letter formation we are declaring, "This is my personal belief system." When we alter specific strokes in our writing, we are simultaneously declaring a change in attitude.

Have you ever seen a sample of handwriting from someone you have never met but felt you knew them because of the way they wrote? Maybe it was a signature in a magazine ad, a politician's signature on a letter, or the writing on an envelope by an anonymous hand. Have you ever felt compelled to show it to someone and say something like, "Wow! Look at that!" and then explain what you had sensed?

A quick and powerful way to find out how personalities are expressed through the pen is to do a simple exercise. Find a three- or four-line sample of writing that is *exactly the opposite* of your own. If your writing slants to the right, find a sample that slants to the left; if you write lightly, find a sample that was written with heavy pressure; if your writing tends to be small, find a sample that is large. If you tend to hug the sides of the page when you write, find a sample with wide margins all around the page. Look at the spacing between the words and the lines and also the direction of the writing line—upward, downward, or straight across the page. If your writing tends to be soft and curly, find a sample that has few loops and is angular in appearance. If it is possible to identify the type of pen used, find that same type of pen. Now, on unlined paper, *copy it exactly*, keeping in mind all of the above factors. Copy it letter for letter, word for word, line for line, being aware of how you are feeling as you copy the words.

Did you just whip right across the page? Or was it an overall frustrating experience? Pretty interesting, isn't it! Keep in mind that your handwriting is as different from the sample you chose to imitate as you are from the person who wrote it. As well as being difficult to copy, you might even have experienced resistance as you moved the pen. Your emotional self may have been whining, "This doesn't feel good!" or "Oh, I hate this!" or "I can't do this!" Physical reactions are also common: a quickening of the heart rate, tightness in the stomach region, quick and shallow breathing, and tension in the shoulders and neck area. You may have found your mind screaming, "Why are you doing this stupid writing thing?!" or— the one I hear most often—"I hate this!" Why all the resistance?

On the mental level, your well-trained thought patterns are rebelling and your body is responding appropriately. Your gut may tighten, your breathing may become shallow, and you may begin to perspire profusely. Your sophisticated inner communication network (comprised of over ten trillion cells) has been eavesdropping on your activity and has set off bells and sirens. "This is not who you are! You cannot write this way! Cease and desist this activity, immediately!" You are out of harmony with your system of beliefs.

Beliefs? Why, of course. Our belief system programs our physiology and therefore directly affects our health. When we worry constantly, acid is poured into the stomach and we get ulcers. When we are laughing and having a good time, our body manufactures interferons (powerful anticancer drugs). When we are frightened, our bodies manufacture extra adrenaline. When we are relaxed and feeling peaceful, our bodies create the identical chemical compound known in the pharmacopoeia as valium.

When you attempt to imitate someone else's handwriting, on a subconscious level you are reaffirming their belief system as your own. With each subtle movement of the pen you are declaring, "This is who I am, how I think, and what I believe," and it becomes quite uncomfortable. Your brain screams in denial. "You can't write that way because that's *not* who you are! Stop! Stop!" The body confirms the anxiety by reacting.

By precisely imitating someone else's handwriting you are attempting to adopt their basic assumptions about life. Pen pressure, angles, dots, spacings, circles, loops, and letter formations are only a few of the thousands of writing characteristics that make our handwriting as personal as our thumbprint and our belief system.

Have you noticed subtle or dramatic changes in your own handwriting through the years? If so, you might want to look back and see what was going on in your life at the time to cause the change. When you switched from writing to printing, or to making any letter in a new way, the reasons you may have attached to the change were most likely irrelevant. "So people can read my writing," "I like the way Suzie Q. makes her s's and I want mine to look that way," or "Printing is faster" are only superficial explanations. When we alter specific strokes or spatial relations in our writing we are also altering, or are in the process of altering, the way we view life.

As we begin to see life differently, we also begin to make choices differently. When we make choices from a place of self-negation, doubt, distrust, or blame, these choices are the product of this inner seeing, this inner belief system. When we choose from a place of honesty, high self-esteem, generosity, and trust, we are simply standing in another place, a place of inner power. Our choices are the result of our attitudes toward life and where we choose to stand. It has nothing at all to do with *who we are,* but rather with *who we see ourselves to be.* And when that viewpoint shifts, everything shifts.

Applied graphotherapy is a behavioral science. Its focus is to interpret and modify writing patterns that directly affect behavior. By introducing self-affirming strokes consistently in handwriting, the writer is introducing the attitudes those strokes reflect and eliminating the opposing ones. By doing so with consistency and intention, the writer creates the possibility of redirecting the course of her or his life in a positive, fulfilling direction. Graphotherapy is one of the most direct, effective, and nonthreatening healing tools known. And what is healing but removing any attitude that says we are not already whole?

One of the most beneficial and long-lasting effects of applied graphotherapy is that the writer becomes intimately involved in her or his own transformational process. The graphotherapist becomes the guide rather than The One Who Knows. The writer assumes personal responsibility in the healing process by taking pen in hand and writing in a specific manner each day. "I am making a difference in my own life" is a phrase I have heard countless times from clients. The healing is literally in the hands of the writer. The steps in the natural process of awakening are not violated, they are only shortened dramatically.

The purpose of this book is to share practical and proven techniques that will enable you to bring desired qualities into your life and to be rid of those that hold you back. This information will enable you to heal on emotional, mental, and spiritual levels. All you need are two notebooks and a pen…and a tenacious commitment to awaken to your own wholeness.

There are two things in life you cannot change: the past and other people. The power of personal transformation lies in changing how you see them. After all, that is what therapy of any kind is about. This possibility unfolds gently yet dramatically as you move your pen intentionally.

Healing is only pen strokes away. If you are the least bit curious, read on. I have written this book for you.

HOW TO USE THIS BOOK

Change Your Handwriting, Change Your Life is designed to be informative, useful, and fun. If you choose to use it as a tool for reshaping your life and achieving direct results, follow these suggestions.

1. Buy two notebooks to be used exclusively for your handwriting exercises.

2. Write in these notebooks every day.

3. Buy a writing pen (ballpoint or fountain are best) of any color. If possible, start with turquoise ink.

4. Incorporate only one handwriting change at a time, for three weeks at a time.

5. Monitor your progress.

Your Notebooks

Each of your two notebooks will serve a separate purpose, so decorate them in order to distinguish between them at a glance. Notebook number one is going to serve as your *Daily Journal*. Notebook number two is your *Dialogue Book*. They both need to be made of unlined paper. If you can find an 8½-by 11-inch notebook already made up with unlined paper, by all means buy it. I have never seen one for sale, however, and if you meet with the same fate, you may want to do what I do. Go to a copy center and ask them to bind enough blank pages to equal a thickness of about 1½ inches. "Wire-O" binding is the most desirable way to bind your notebook: it allows the pages to turn easily and it does not uncurl like plastic comb-binding. It is important to have this book bound on the wide, 11-inch side, because this page orientation will give you free wrist action with either hand, as you will be writing longways.

This is your notebook and nobody else's, so, if you wish, choose your favorite colors for paper as an alternative to white. Be sure to ask for cardstock front and back covers in your very favorite colors. Using the hand you usually don't write with (your nondominant hand), use crayons or colored pens to claim these books as your own by writing "(*Your first name*)'s Writing Book" across the front cover of each notebook. To complement your name, draw a picture of yourself. Do all this with your nondominant hand. Be free and open. Draw yourself as you want to be. Don't worry about how it looks. Have it be the way *you* say you want it to be, and not the way someone else says. This book is for you, and is not being created in order to earn the approval of anyone except you. Once that is done, these books are yours.

Your Pen

Buy a pen you like to write with. When you go pen shopping, bring a pad of paper with you so you can try out each pen you take a fancy to. Draw pictures with it. Write with it. Make sure you like the way it looks. Hold it in your hand, turn it around a few times, then write a few words with it on your paper pad. Make sure you like *everything* about the pen before you buy it—*everything*—the weight, the way it feels between your fingers, the texture and thickness of the barrel, the nib size if it's a fountain pen, and the point width if it's a ballpoint. Be especially aware of the color of ink. Select your favorite: not the color your fourth grade teacher said to use, not the color your mother or your best friend likes best, but *your* favorite color of ink—the color that you like to see your words become as they flow onto the paper.

Let's Get Started

This book is arranged by Quality. Use the table of contents to see which quality you would like to bring into your life, then turn to that page. The exercises that accompany each quality are designed to give you maximum benefit as quickly as possible as you begin your new writing habits. By performing them exactly, you can create a direct path to the attitudinal change you are pursuing.

Set Up and Use Your Daily Journal.

- Put today's date in the upper right-hand corner of the first inside page of your Daily Journal. Continue dating each page consecutively in the upper right-hand corner until you have numbered three weeks' worth of days.

- At the top and in the center of the first page, write the personal *Declaration To My Wholeness* that corresponds to the Quality you have chosen. Write it with firm intention, incorporating your new letter change. Be sure to memorize the declaration and repeat it silently many times throughout the day, especially in circumstances that call it forth from you. Think it. Absorb it. Be it. Use your words wisely and use them mindfully. Use them to design a masterpiece! Words spoken or written with intention and willpower carve your future. What you *say* will be, *will be*. Be very sure you want what you are asking for, because *you will get it*.

An affirmation is what it implies: It affirms what you say. A declaration goes beyond mere affirmation. When you create a statement as a declaration, the intention within and behind it intensifies its power and, in effect, stakes your words deeply into the ground, claiming them as your commitment to life and to yourself. This commitment becomes uniquely yours. This energy *uses you* and calls you forth into it. The feeling that goes with a powerful declaration is, "I have spoken, therefore it is so." Ask carefully. Be attentive and purposeful. Then claim it as your own.

- About two thirds of the way down each page, draw a line across the page. Don't use a ruler. Be bold. Do it freehand!

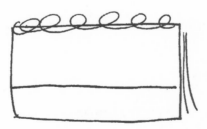

- Copy the practice paragraph that corresponds with the quality you have chosen and complete the exercise that follows it. Once you know which handwriting change you will be making, fill one page each day, using your dominant hand (the hand you ordinarily write with) to write about whatever comes into your mind, incorporating the desired change in your handwriting. Write about taxes, climbing up mountains, composing music, baking bread… anything at all that you gather from your feelings. Above all, other than the initial test paragraph for the quality, don't copy what anyone else has written. This is your book. These are your thoughts. These are your feelings. You are the author! You don't have to worry about spelling, punctuation, grammar, or even continuity. No one else is going to see this book. So have fun, be yourself, and just write!

- When your writing reaches the line that you have drawn across the page, stop. Put your pen down. Close your eyes. Take a few deep breaths. Now open your eyes and pick up the pen with your nondominant hand and fill up the bottom third of the page describing what it *felt* like when you altered the stroke formation(s). Comments such as these may arise: "This is really uncomfortable," "I was feeling really irritable," "My writing looked prettier the way I used to write,"or "This new stroke looks weird."

The resistance that is speaking through your nondominant hand is the voice of the attitude you are beginning to replace. It has an energy as real as the pen you are moving and your eyes that watch the words appear. It was put in place many years ago and has been with you a long time. The new stroke you are beginning to write has set off a warning alarm directed toward this attitude to let it know that its days are numbered. The greater the resistance you feel to changing a specific writing habit, the longer that trait has lived within you and the stronger a foothold it has. Expect resistance.

Let's say you've decided to incorporate the quality of **Forgiveness** into your writing. This causes the quality of **Harsh Judgment** to fight for its life within you as you begin to create this new change in your life. If given a voice, it might protest: "But I have protected you all these years from opening your heart to other people, and I have helped you keep all those sharp angles in your writing, not to mention the tight spacing and connectedness within words. And look at the hook in that *c*. It was hard work to get you to write that way. If you change all of this, we will be completely vulnerable. I did what you wanted and now you are telling me I did a bad job. Please don't write this new way. Each time you do, I feel like I'm dying, and I can't breathe! Please don't kill me. I did the best I knew how."

Resistance, disbelief, anger, mistrust, and terror are common reactions. **Harsh Judgment**, in this example, is fighting for its survival. As these feelings rise to the surface and the internal conversations begin, just be with them. Close your eyes, embrace your feelings gently, rock them in your arms, hum to them gently, and be with them. Just be with them. Note the physical reactions within your body.

- Write down your feelings in your second notebook, your Dialogue Book. Write with your nondominant hand. This is the hand in which your unexpressed feelings reside. Let them out. Let them all out on the paper. Give them a space to express themselves freely and without censure.

Using your new handwriting change with your dominant hand, write to **Harsh Judgment**, addressing it as though it were a living, breathing being, for indeed it is. Reassure it that it *has* done a good job, a splendid one, in fact, because you have such trouble being truly forgiving! Let it know that *because* it has done such a good job and is so reliable, you are inviting it to take on a *new* job: that of a supporting role in bringing the quality of **Forgiveness** into your life by helping you change your writing habits. State lovingly and firmly that it may take on the new job or not. But if it chooses not to assist you, then it will die, for you have made the conscious choice to be a person who no longer judges harshly. Then put your pen in your nondominant hand and let **Harsh Judgment** reply. Keep up the dialogue as long as you'd like.

When you are through, use your dominant hand to draw a picture of what you think **Harsh Judgment** looks like. Then with your nondominant hand, draw a picture of **Forgiveness**. Quiet your mind, speak from your heart, and let your feelings spill out freely. Draw. Write. Listen. Be.

Use your Dialogue Book to create an ongoing dialogue with the resistant quality whenever you like, using your dominant hand to be the listener responding to the emotional reactions of your nondominant hand.

What To Expect As You Change Your Handwriting

When you make a firm commitment to change your handwriting, and thereby your attitudes, you put into motion the *Principle of Intention and Commitment*, one of the most powerful allies to have at your side once you are committed to personal transformation. I have seen it explode into action again and again in the lives of my clients, and I continue to experience its effects in my own life. Very simply, it is this: **Once the commitment to claim your wholeness is firmly in place and you begin to alter strokes in your handwriting as a result of this commitment, you will be given immediate and intimate opportunities to prove your intention.**

Here is a common example. Let us say you have an issue with your mother (living or dead). She abused you when your were young, or she is always telling you what to do, or you feel that you can never do anything right in her eyes. The first step toward healing this relationship is to realize that you cannot change her. Period. Bottom line. From that place, the next step is to affirm, "I want to be at peace with my mother. I want to be able to look at her and know that she has provided me with the lessons I have had to learn, and that she is (has been) the perfect mother for me. I want to be filled with a sense of gratitude each time I think of her. Since I can't change her or anything she has done or continues to do, I am willing to change my attitude toward her." That, in the form of a commitment, begins instantly to clear a path for healing to occur.

Once you have selected a stroke change and you begin to practice it attentively on a daily basis, here's what will happen. Either your mother will unexpectedly move a block away from you, or virtually every woman you meet will begin to remind you of her: your boss, your best friend, your neighbor, even the woman at the check-out stand at the local supermarket. Once your intention is clearly stated and you put out the willingness to heal from *your* end of the relationship by incorporating that new stroke or spacing formation into your writing, you are accepting responsibility for your part in the healing process. An unseen energy extends out from the pen in a direct line to the Universe and says, "I'm ready to clean this one up." The Universe simply takes you at your word. The person with whom you are at odds will begin to appear in the faces and attitudes of other people in your life. Everywhere! I have never seen this fail. You might want to experiment to see what happens. This Truth does not vary.

The letters of the alphabet are sacred symbols, each with its own deep intrinsic meaning, each with both its clear and shadow sides, just like us. They represent the complexity of human personality traits and their interactions. When you begin altering strokes, letters, or spacing in your writing, do it consciously. Attentively. With the quality the Buddhists call "mindfulness." Pay attention to the new writing change you are beginning to use and create an intimate working relationship between your mind, your heart, and your pen. Keep a *Log of Miracles*.

Log of Miracles

First of all, let's define *miracle*. A miracle is not some outlandish, impractical, cosmic occurrence. A miracle is the result of having put out intentional energy to attract what appears to be impossible. The key component of any miracle is *commitment*. You can't have one without the other.

Commitment generates an energy all its own and draws to it what it needs in order to expand. It is difficult for the mind to understand a miracle, because the mind does not go beyond the principle of cause and effect into the forbidden territory beyond. Miracles stretch beyond logical boundaries and leave the mind in the dust. They are real, concrete, and to be expected in your life—if you live from commitment.

If changing your handwriting as a means of changing your attitude toward life still sounds a bit suspect to you, or if you are simply curious to prove or disprove its impact, make it a point to keep your Log of Miracles faithfully. What harm can it do? Besides, it's easy. Here's how.

On the reverse side of your daily writing page, write at the top, (*Your first name*)'s Log of Miracles. Each time a miracle occurs, write it down. A short and direct sentence is all you need. It could read something like this: "I saw my ex-wife today and felt a deep compassion for her without wanting to change anything about her," or "Today I spoke to someone who I previously found intimidating, and we had a warm and friendly discussion." Next to the miracle, write down the specific writing change you are working on, the date you began practicing it, and the date the miracle occurred.

By definition, a miracle is something that had no way of happening, considering the current direction of events in your life. By keeping this ongoing log, you will begin to see clearly the impact you are having on your own life by consistently making specific writing changes.

THE FIVE NOBLE TRUTHS
OF GRAPHOTHERAPY

There are several vital premises to keep in mind as you begin to explore the fascinating topic called "My Written Self." I call them *The Five Noble Truths of Graphotherapy.*

I have listed them separately so that you may find them easily and consult them often. As you begin to use your handwriting as a window into your subconscious, your tendency may be to judge yourself harshly. Negative judgment comes from fear. By referring to these *Five Noble Truths* repeatedly, you will be able to polish your window free of fear and see through the clear pane of compassion and understanding.

1. In people, as in handwriting, there is no such thing as good, bad, right, or wrong. Those four qualities are merely opinions and hold no weight at all in working with the precious commodity called "Myself." Who you are is who you are. What you do is what you do. Evaluation of either of these is only a matter of personal interpretation, and as such, is without value, except to the one who holds on to it.

2. The frequency with which a writing habit occurs in your writing is the frequency with which the quality it represents occurs in your life. If you see certain stroke placements and formations now and again, the trait they represent occurs only now and again in your life. If there are consistently repeated patterns in your writing, there is a direct correlation between them and the consistency with which the traits they represent occur in your life.

3. In looking at the handwriting of someone with whom you are in a relationship, both your own and the other person's handwriting are required if you want to find out how buttons are getting pushed and what is activating them. **Remember Noble Truth #1**.

4. The degree of difficulty in the mastery of a stroke change is directly proportional to the value it will have in your life: The greater the difficulty, the greater the value.

5. Once the commitment to claim your wholeness is firmly in place and you begin to alter strokes in your handwriting, you will be given immediate and intimate opportunities to prove your intention. The moment you use your pen to declare that you are now willing to complete an issue in your life, this issue will confront you clearly and immediately in the form of a person, a situation, or a relationship.

These Truths do not vary.

CHAPTER TWO

Honesty

Honesty is being totally vulnerable,

and once we have achieved that,

we can never be hurt...

· Anonymous ·

DECLARATION TO MY WHOLENESS

I have nothing to hide.

I speak truthfully from my

healing voice at all times.

AT BIRTH WE HAVE two tiny feet unencumbered by any covering, with toes that are free to stretch, curl, and wiggle. At about the age of two or three—or earlier, depending on our family situation—we put a shoe on each of those feet and we walk through life. These shoes have names: one is called "looking good," the other, "being right." As we take one step after another, these well-polished shoes leave prints that mark our course in life, creating our relationships, our decisions, and our interactions on all levels. How we interpret honesty often depends which foot we're standing on at the moment.

Honesty is the willingness to remove those confining shoes and stand in our bare feet, just as we are, with nothing to hide; to honor all of our past and to forgive our mistakes and shortcomings; and to acknowledge with equal clarity our strengths, our abilities, and our talents. From that **place** we can create a foundation upon which to build our lives. **Honesty** means always speaking to the God within the other person, just as we appreciate their speaking to the God within us. **Honesty** is not to be confused with the "facts," knowing that facts are often bent and gnarled from our interpretation of them. To speak honestly is to speak in such a way that our words are never injurious, but a source of grace and healing for both ourself and the person to whom we are speaking.

But **Honesty** does not stop there. It stretches beyond the boundaries of simply telling the truth and embraces integrity. Like a body without a heart, without the one, the other cannot exist.

I define integrity as that quality which prevents us from doing, acting, thinking, or saying anything that conflicts with our value system. To some it may imply keeping one's word. When teamed with **Honesty**, it shifts in depth to encompass *being* your word. When you make an appointment, do you write it on your calendar in ink or pencil? Do you return all phone calls? Do you answer all letters? Do you discuss your differences with the person you are upset with, or just blame them without speaking to them? Do you acknowledge your own mistakes and learn from them? Do you tell lies? Do you gossip? Are you dependable? When you say you will do something, do you do it?

Let's do a spot check.

PRACTICE

Copy this paragraph in your Daily Journal.

Only the trusting can afford honesty, for only they can see its value. Honesty does not apply only to what you say. The term actually means consistency. There is nothing you say that contradicts what you think or do; no thought opposes any other thought; no act belies your word; and no word lacks agreement with another. Such are the truly honest. At no level are they in conflict with themselves. Therefore it is impossible for them to be in conflict with anyone or anything.

A Course in Miracles

Look at your *a*'s and *o*'s. Are they compressed and vertical-looking?

#1 not apply

Or round and full?   *#2*   *not apply*

Do they have inner loops? If so, on which side?

The left   *#3*   *a o*   or the right?   *#4*   *a o*

Are they open at the top   *#5*   *ʊ ʊ*   or closed?   *#6*   *o o*

It all makes a difference. Look carefully. Use a highlighter pen to mark what you see.

Now look at these *a*'s and *o*'s.

#7   *anyone or anything*

These full ovals are clearly drawn with no inner loops of any kind. Practice writing a few of them, forming the circle beginning at the top. How does it feel? Do a few more. Now write the practice paragraph once again, this time slowly and deliberately, drawing your *a*'s and *o*'s clearly and loop-free like those in example #7. If this is a new stroke for you, observe your mental, emotional, and physical reactions as you write. Using your nondominant hand, write these reactions at the bottom of your practice page. Take four or five lines to do this.

Loops are always containers in handwriting; where they occur determines what they contain. Although they are appropriate in certain letters, they do not belong in *a, o, d, g,* and *q* (the *communication letters*), because they serve as hiding places. Where they occur, and in which letter, determines what you are hiding and whether you are hiding things about yourself or about others.

If inner loops occur on the inner left, you are hiding things about

yourself from others.　*#8*

If they occur on the inner right,　*#9*

you are keeping things hidden about others. Depending on other hand-writing patterns, if a small inner loop occurs on the right of the *o,* it can also mean that you keep confidences well.

If inner loops occur consistently on both left and right sides at the

same time,　*#10*

you have difficulty being frank, and telling the truth is not a well-developed habit for you. If you are concealing something about your past, the truth can even terrify you. The nature of this reaction—whether it is deliber-ate and calculated or the result of fear—will show up in other writing patterns.

A loop-free circle does not mean a person always tells the truth, however. People who lie consistently can make circle letters without inner loops, usually in printing or print-script. Their propensity for avoiding the truth will show up in other writing patterns.

One circle letter I suggest you look for is this: *#11*

If you look carefully, you will see that the entire letter is encircled by the introductory stroke. It scoops it up and completely embraces it.

If you have this stroke in your writing, you might want to begin practicing all your circle letters by consciously starting them at the top of the circle.

#12 *a o d g g*

Write a few lines for practice. The particular letter formation in example #11 (in relation to other strokes in the handwriting) most often points to a secret about the past that is being held on to for dear life, fearful that someone will find out about it. If you have this stroke, yet want to be at peace with your secret and be able to speak of it without shame or embarrassment, begin with this letter change. Once you have it mastered, I promise you that other letter formations in your writing will also change to reflect a new freedom from the past. **Remember Noble Truth #4**: *The greater the difficulty, the greater the value.*

CHAPTER THREE

Listening

While the Clear mind

listens to a bird singing,

the Stuffed-Full-of-Knowledge-

and-Cleverness mind wonders

what kind of bird is singing.

· Benjamin Hoff ·

DECLARATION TO MY WHOLENESS

With a still mind and an open heart,

I listen to everyone receptively.

HOW DO YOU LISTEN? Do you listen with the intent to hear what is being communicated, or just to say how *you* see the issue being discussed? Are you able to set aside your own viewpoint, whether you agree or disagree, and just listen . . . silently, receptively— and be completely present and attentive? Compassionate and open? Clear **Listening** is a rare and treasured gift. Have you ever received it? If so, you probably still remember the occasion and the person who gave it to you! It's pretty rare, truly a priceless treasure. Would you like to listen clearly?

If you find it difficult to listen without hearing through the knowing-how-it-is filter, especially in the dynamic of a spouse-spouse, parent-child, or boss-employee relationship, you might want to bring the quality of **Listening** into your life. Still your busy mind, drop gently into your heart, and listen from there. Listen beyond the words being spoken to their source inside the speaker. There are only two places inside us to listen or speak from: our mind and our heart. There are no other places in there. Knowing that, be conscious of where you listen from. From our heart we listen clearly and openly. When we are in our minds, however, opinions create so much background noise that we cannot listen. Only we can choose where to stand.

True **Listening** can become a source of strength in all of your relationships. You may be surprised to find that the people you begin listening to treat you with more respect, and that negative conversations are more easily and quickly resolved. When you make it a habit to listen to your children, friends, employers, employees, coworkers, or neighbors, they may startle you by a willingness to be greater than you ever imagined.

To listen is to be there for someone attentively without speaking. Not to agree. Not to disagree. Above all, not to advise. Just to be there, completely present. Silent. Honoring. Bite your tongue, quiet your mind, then open your heart and **Listen**. Just **Listen**.

PRACTICE

Copy this paragraph in your Daily Journal.

> *Empathic [from empathy] listening is powerful because it gives you accurate data to work with. Instead of projecting your own autobiography and assuming thoughts, feelings, motives and interpretation, you're dealing with the reality inside another person's head and heart. You're listening to understand. You're focused on receiving the deep communication of another human soul.... When you listen with empathy to another person, you give that person psychological air.... This need for psychological air impacts communication in every area of life.*

> *Stephen R. Covey*

Hold the page away from you and observe it as an X-ray of your nonphysical body. What does the spacing look like? Are the words placed close together?

#13 listening is powerful because

Or are they far apart?   *#14*

it gives you accurate

The average spacing between words is the width of your normal letter *a*. The word spacing will tell you what kind of distance you prefer to put between yourself and others.

Are the letters cramped and tight?

#15 *of another human soul*

Or are they open and full?   #16

of another human soul

This indicates your degree of self-expression. Oddly enough, persons with tight writing tend to talk a great deal, almost as a defense against having to listen. As we all know, when we are talking, we can't listen! Compressed writers tend to be closed to any ideas but their own.

Does the writing predominantly have angles?

#17 *you give that*

(Not much softness there!)
Does it mostly flow with soft, curved strokes?

#18 *you give that*

(Laps and hugs abound.)
What do your *e*'s look like? Are the loops open or closed?

#19 *because because*

Think of "ear" when you consider the *e*. This letter reflects how open or closed you are to listening. Are they fairly spacious and soft?

#20 *interpretation*

If so, you give others the space to speak and are not harsh in your assessment of what they say or believe.

Are the tops diagonal?

#21 *head and heart*

This is a rare phenomenon, but it does occur. If you make your *e*'s like this consistently, you probably hear yourself saying, "That would never work," or "That's the silliest idea I've ever heard."

All of the above questions relate to empathy, tolerance, and the gift of **Listening**. The appearance of the letter *e* will give you a clue as to how open or closed the writer is to listening. A slim loop represents the writer who listens *behind* what is being said rather than to the surface words, but if your *e*'s are generally closed, you might want to look at the overall appearance of your writing to see if your mind is closed also. The rest of the writing will give definite clues. If you decide to open up your *e*'s and leave space in the loop, you might also decide to incorporate garlands wherever you can.

A garland looks like this: *#22*

communication

Think of placing a garland of flowers around someone's neck in friendship when you think of this shape. Or think of a garland as a hand reaching out to hold someone else's hand, just as the ending stroke reaches out to the next word. It is a friendly, welcoming gesture. Drawn consistently, garlands encourage the love of freely giving as well as freely receiving. Your heart will begin to overflow with a warm sense of acknowledgment once you begin using garlands and open-loop *e*'s. Together they will shake free any stinginess in your heart and help loosen it up. You will begin to hear others from a new depth of caring and empathy.

Above all, draw your *t* crossbars firmly, balanced on the stem and placed high.

#23

This will solidify your self-image and you will have no need to defend yourself with the shield of "knowing" because you will not feel attacked when others disagree with you. You may even begin to see disagreement as an opportunity to broaden your knowledge and understanding.

By creating a sense of spaciousness on the written page, you will begin doing the same in your life. Words represent other people, and spacing between words, lines, or letters, indicates the kind of space you allow them. It's best not to cramp your words, lines, or letters. Open up your writing and just let it all breathe.

Stop here for a moment. *You* breathe. Close your eyes. Inhale deeply. Hold the breath. Exhale with a long *huhhhhhh* sound. Let it all out. A little more. Do it again. *Really* inhale, like it's the last breath you have. Draw it in. More. More. Now exhale fully, deliberately, and slowly with a sound that lets the world know that you are exhaling.

Now that is what I mean when I say, "Open up your writing." As your writing begins to breathe, so do you. By breathing fully and with attention you begin to give yourself the space to be—to just be. In doing so, you also begin to allow others the same kind of freedom. Breathe. Often and deeply. Mindfully. And let it all go. Then open your heart and listen.

CHAPTER FOUR

Self-Discipline

When Discipline was a teenager

too poor to afford dance lessons,

she skipped lunch to pay

for her lessons.

· J. Ruth Gendler ·

DECLARATION TO MY WHOLENESS

I willingly embrace my commitments

in life and joyfully accept my part

in having them realized.

W HEN MOST OF US hear the word *self-discipline*, we cringe from the weight of it. Let's take the phrase apart in order to see it from a new shudder-free perspective. Rather than experiencing the weight of punishment or burden, let's walk into the word and see what lives there: the word *disciple*. A disciple to what? You are a disciple of your own life, your own being as Self. **Self-discipline** is learning life's lessons in order to claim your own power, your own magnificence, your own uniqueness. It is to harness willingly and joyfully, your mind and your will, and train them to dance with your best intentions rather than allowing them to choreograph their own mischief and excuses. You may even begin to see **Self-discipline** as the bottom line for being in training for Life, as a strong foundation upon which to build everything you want for yourself and for others.

When you make friends with **Self-discipline**, you begin ridding yourself of habits that undermine your health on all levels. For example, on the physical level: quitting smoking or overeating; on the emotional level: holding back a quick temper and thinking before you speak; on the mental level: setting time aside to read good books rather than watch TV; and on the spiritual level: to draw into your life some desired spiritual practice. Maybe you've wanted to learn to meditate, read more spiritual books, or simply spend more time hiking or just "being" in the backwoods with nature, but you say that life's responsibilities have you trapped and won't let you go. You may hear the words "I just don't have time" spill out of your mouth. **Self-discipline** is the quality that says "yes" to what you really want and spurs you on to do what is required to achieve it.

PRACTICE

Copy this paragraph in your Daily Journal.

> *One of basketball's prime tenets is discipline. You must maintain it.... There is no replacement for sound funda-mentals and strict discipline. They will reinforce you in the toughest circumstance. The importance of little things cannot be over-emphasized—like double-tying the shoestrings; seeing that uniforms and shoes are properly fitted; and forming the habit, based on the assumption that every shot will be missed, of getting your hands above your shoulders when a shot is taken so you can come down with the rebound.*

John Wooden

Look at your paragraph, especially at your *t* crossbars. These are

t stems   #24

and these are *t crossbars*.   #25

The stems of the letter *t* reflect a pride and dignity in one's profes-sion. Crossbars are the *willpower strokes*. It is a conservative estimate to say that there are hundreds of thousands of ways to make *t* stems and crossbars, and each combination indicates something subtly different. Most of us have a variety of *t* formations in our writing. The letter *t* has to do with goal-setting, self-image, self-esteem, and belief in one's abilities to achieve. The crossbar is an indicator of the willpower behind those qualities. Look at it as a chinning bar: the kind of bar that you reach up to and grab, then pull yourself up to so your feet leave the floor. When you exert yourself and stretch high enough you are able to put your chin on it. That's the *t* crossbar. Every time you see the letter *t*, remember this image. How high do you set your goals? Do you set them within reach, or way up there where you have to stretch, pull, and expand to reach them? Do your feet leave the floor? The *height* of your *t* crossbar reflects this.

#26

What degree of effort are you willing to put behind your projects and your dreams? The *weight* of the crossbar comes in here.

#27

Do you begin with firm intentions and then peter out?

#28

Do you start and finish with gusto?

#29

Do you put off doing things until the last minute?

#30

Do you infuse your life with enthusiasm?

#31

Or with a lukewarm attitude?

#32

Do you have an issue with needing to be in control?

#33

Your *t* crossbar will direct you to those answers.

When you incorporate **Self-discipline** into your life, you are taking your will off autopilot and putting yourself at the controls. Rather than acting from habit, you are making the decision to act consciously. There is one powerfully transforming *t* crossbar that can stop you from acting unthinkingly because it causes you to bend your will to do what you want, and not what past habits dictate. It looks simple to do, and it is … the first few times. Here is what it looks like.

#34

It is called the *umbrella t.*

Under the paragraph you just copied, write a few of these *umbrella t*'s then begin writing words that include them. As you begin to write them again and again, there is an excellent possibility that you will feel impatient, irritated, and annoyed. Quite annoyed. The reaction that is commonly felt is, "You're not going to tell *me* what to do!" because you are replacing an unconscious habit with intentional action. "What do you mean I can't have another cookie (or cigarette, or drink)?" Dialoguing with the resistance can be a dramatic and revealing exercise, because what often surfaces are conversations from childhood or adolescence that have been neither safely expressed nor listened to.

By writing with both right and left hands in your Dialogue Book, you can achieve the full impact of this particular letter change and unearth many old, unspoken conversations. You will discover the age of the child who is resisting the soul gift of **Self-discipline**. I promise you, it isn't your mature adult self!

CHAPTER FIVE

Enthusiasm

Nothing great was ever achieved

without enthusiasm.

· Ralph Waldo Emerson ·

DECLARATION TO MY WHOLENESS

I am fearless and free and share my

Inner Light with all whom I meet.

ENTHUSIASM AND EXCITEMENT live in separate rooms inside of us, yet we often use them interchangeably. Excitement comes from the outer husk of us and is temporary and short-lived. It is a product of the ego self and lives in our emotions. Fluctuating and unpredictable, it comes and goes depending on our mood or feeling at any given time. It can be quite fickle.

The word *enthusiasm,* with its roots in Greek, literally means "infused with God": it is a quality of the soul. We all have it. It does not express itself in frenzied activity or with the shaking of pom-poms, tambourines, or sermonizing fists. Like white-hot coals burning in the belly of a furnace, it is a constant and available source of fuel within each one of us. We can either fan it to life and use it or continually dampen it with the hope that it will go away.

I have a treasured friend who is a living, breathing example of **Enthusiasm**. He is enchantingly unassuming and gracious, brilliant and humble, and one of the kindest persons I have ever met. He is one of the few persons I know who shows respect equally to everyone he meets. **Enthusiasm** stokes his soul. He is afraid of almost nothing, including what others think of him, and he is completely at peace with who he is and who he is not. His every word and movement are joyful manifestations of untethered **Enthusiasm**, and life for him is an adventure in progress. He was my instructor at Stanford University, and the parameters he set for the class shattered tradition. "The purpose of learning is not just to know. It is to be fluid and spontaneous, alert and attentive. Your homework is to keep a written account of how you are *living* what you are learning. Translate this class into you life! *Be* it!" And we lived and we wrote. And did we learn!

It is not so much his personality that inspires people, as it is the quality of **Enthusiasm** in his soul that touches everyone around him like a magic wand. When you're around Jeffrey you *know* that you're great! He wouldn't have it any other way.

Enthusiasm is both nonintrusive yet compelling. It possesses a magnetism all its own that lives deep within the human soul and draws others into its vortex of uplifting energy. It has a clear and expectant attitude that awakens you to who you really are, and suddenly you find yourself being the person you only dreamed you could be, doing things that you had seen as completely unimaginable, out of the question, and quite impractical. And there you are . . . doing them and loving every minute of it. **Enthusiasm**. A God-spark ignited!

PRACTICE

Copy this paragraph in your Daily Journal.

Having carefully observed people over many years, I am convinced that the fortunate individuals who achieve the most in life are invariably activated by enthusiasm. The men who do the most with their lives are those who approach human existence, its opportunities and its problems—even its rough moments—with a confident attitude and an enthusiastic point of view. Therefore, it seems timely to stress the vital power of enthusiasm and to suggest procedures to develop and maintain this powerful and precious motivating force.... Enthusiasm can truly make a difference—the difference in how your life will turn out.

Norman Vincent Peale

Go back and look at two things in your writing: first, the crossbars on your *t* stems, and second, *downstrokes* such as in the *m* and *n,* and in the *b* and *k.* Here are examples of downstrokes and how they are made.

#35

First of all, make sure that your vertical *t* stem is about two- to two-and-a-half times the height of the small letter *a* and that there is no loop in it.

#36

Either retrace it   #37

or simply draw it like a stick from top to bottom.   #38

Retraced *upstrokes* are desirable. In a well-drawn *t* they reflect pride in accomplishment.

Now let's look at the crossbars. How high have you placed them? Did you draw them firmly or gently? For this exercise it is especially important to notice how *long* they are. Your willpower lives in the *t* crossbar. It will tell you immediately whether you mean what you say or whether you are just talking wistfully about what *could* be. If you want to infuse your statements with the power of intention to fulfill, practice your *t* crossbars faithfully.

Remember, the *t* crossbar is the willpower stroke: the chinning bar for goal-setting. The height indicates how far the writer is willing to stretch in order to achieve. It also indicates the writer's self-esteem: the belief in their ability to achieve. Crossed at the top of the Mid Zone, it will keep superior achievements and self-esteem in check. (To read about the importance of zones, see page 140.) The writer who feels comfortable crossing his *t*s low is not willing to stretch beyond her or his comfort zone or to achieve where others have failed. I strongly recommend crossing all *t*s firmly on the stem, placed high, and in a slightly tilted direction from the lower left to upper right. This type of *t* crossbar clearly states, "I can accomplish anything I put my mind to, and I will!"

#39

If you want to experience magnetic enthusiasm in all areas of your life and draw others into supporting your ideas, begin to write your *t* crossbars with the following points in mind:

- Place your crossbars very high on a tall unlooped *t* stem.

#40

- Draw them heavily, beginning and ending them bluntly. This affirms positive determination.

#41

- Above all, make them enduring, i.e., long and sweeping.

#42

Draw them with your soul energy, not just your fingers and pen. Really draw them. When you begin moving that pen across the paper, press down so the paper pays attention! Impress it!

Because retraced downstrokes reinforce the repression of any kind of creativity, I will mention them in regard to several qualities in this book. A stroke that often accompanies retraced downstrokes is called a *reining-in stroke.*

#43   𝓂   𝓃   𝓃

You can feel the restraint just by looking at the letters. It reflects the energy of a writer who is kicking the horse madly and at the same time pulling back tightly on the reins of expressive, creative freedom. Does this sound familiar? Retraced downstrokes in the Mid Zone combined with reining-in strokes are considered red flags. They are an affront to the human soul because they block personal creativity from expression. By drawing light, short *t* bars, retracing your downstrokes and reining-in consistently, you will be pregnant with dreams and creative abilities all of your life but will never give birth! These are sure signs that you are repressing your spontaneity, creativity, and untapped potential. It's not that you don't *have* spontaneity, creativity, or potential. But when you incorporate these strokes consistently, you hold yourself back from *expressing* your innermost dreams, ideas, and giving them the unique flavor only you can lend. You may talk a lot about what you are going to do or who you are going to become, but these strokes will guarantee that your intentions will remain only talk. Your potential will remain well hidden. It will never see the light of day.

So you want to give birth to your own uniqueness? In addition to flowing *t* crossbars, do this:

#44   𝓂   𝓃   𝓀   𝓀

These are called *pull-away strokes* because, by pulling away from the downstroke, you are giving yourself permission to pull away from the "shoulds" of old conditioning and to create a space for your specialness to shine. We will talk more about these in the quality section **Willingness to Risk**.

These are *reining-out strokes,*

#45

so called because they give the reins some slack and grant permission for your dreams to explore undiscovered territories of the imagination. If your writing reflects reining-in strokes and retraced downstrokes in the Mid Zone, write in your notebook using both pull-away and reining-out strokes. Go slowly, writing just a few letters at first, then try a few words. Finally, fill a few lines with writing. See how it feels. Now do some more. Open up the starting gate and let your creativity run free. Any resistance you feel is simply your old habit of holding back.

If you tend to stay in the background when you're just dying to speak your mind, these stroke changes can alter how others see you because you will find yourself sharing what *you* feel. You may even surprise yourself, right in front of everybody! **Enthusiasm** is a God-spark inside each of us. If you want to feed your soul, keep that spark alive, and draw out the **Enthusiasm** that lives deep within. Give yourself permission to express who you are by drawing your *t* crossbars with firm intention, convert all retraces to pull-away strokes, and consistently write reining-out strokes. Do your homework daily and attentively, and within just a few weeks, you will be witness to a miracle. In fact, you will be the miracle!

CHAPTER SIX

Forgiveness

If you forgive people enough,

you belong to them and they to you,

whether either person likes it or not—

squatter's rights of the heart.

· James Hilton ·

DECLARATION TO MY WHOLENESS

Today, and only today,

I will perceive everyone who crosses my path

as perfectly innocent of any wrongdoing.

I CAN THINK OF NO other concept as misunderstood as **Forgiveness**. My upbringing was in a Christian household in which forgiveness was a way of life. If someone broke your toy, hit you, or in any other way disturbed you, you forgave them. Instead of expressing anger or any other outgoing emotion, I was taught to cover it gently with **Forgiveness**. If I cried or became upset, *I* was the wrongdoer, and the one I was supposed to forgive became the good guy. I came to believe that **Forgiveness** was something one does as a means of making the pain okay and of making people like you. Although it was childish thinking, it ruled my life well into adulthood.

It was not until I had been divorced for twelve years that I learned intimately what **Forgiveness** really was. I was leading a seminar on "Forgiveness" when, toward the end of the day, some words started spilling out of my mouth that stopped me and literally paralyzed my speech. For the life of me, I don't remember what they were, but I clearly remember what they did. It was as though someone outside of me was fed up with what I was saying and suddenly shouted inside my head, *"Time out. Wait a minute. Enough is enough.* Forget all of those books you've read and be HONEST. *You've never forgiven anyone in your life!"* In mid-sentence, I became mute. I felt my face flushing, my palms became sweaty, and in those few seconds that felt like an hour, I regained my composure and muttered, "Let's take a fifteen-minute break."

What had become very clear to me in that *Aha!* experience was that I had never truly, from my heart, forgiven my ex-husband. When I left him years before, I had seen him as an inadequate father and husband, and when we parted I told him that I forgave him everything. I truly thought I had. In that one flash of insight, the scenario shifted and I realized what I had really done: rather than forgiving him, I had made him very, very wrong and I had walked away as righteous as hell.

I was dumbfounded! Not only that, but, like a dying person reviewing their life in an instant, every relationship in which I thought I had forgiven someone flashed before my eyes as though it were on a movie screen. The voice was right. *I had never forgiven anyone in my life!* In that millisecond I saw very clearly that I had repeated the same pattern each time. I made *them* wrong, and I became the one who was right.

That evening I called my ex-husband. Since we were rarely in touch, he was surprised.

"Are you okay?" was his first question.

"Oh, I'm fine, thanks. You?"

"I'm fine too."

"Well," I continued, "I just want to let you know that when we separated in '77 I told you I forgave you, and I thought I had. I realized only today that I have never really done that."

He was still for a moment, then replied, "I'm not sure I know what you're talking about."

"I'm calling to let you know that I never really forgave you at all. I made you very wrong and I made me very right. I didn't see it at the time, but now it is as clear as day. I'm calling to let you know that you're absolutely perfect the way you are and that you never, ever have to change. And that I love you a lot."

An uneasy silence suspended itself shakily between us. "Are you sure you're okay?" was his response.

"Please believe me, I've never felt better in my whole life."

He responded testily, "And you say you love me?"

"Exactly as you are," I replied, "and I have a favor to ask of you."

"Oh yeah. What's that?"

Taking a deep breath from the bottom of my heart, I quietly responded "Will you please forgive me?"

Freedom, like wings, sprouted inside of me and I experienced such a lightness of heart that I felt I could fly. I had never been present to such a sensation in my entire life.

What were the two cement blocks that had fallen from my heart? They were negative judgment and the expectations that had never been fulfilled. I realized that I had not been upset with *him* all of those years. What I had been upset about was the person I expected him to be, how I wanted him to think, and the direction in which I wanted him to grow. He simply had not fulfilled my expectations. It had nothing to do with him, personally. It had everything to do with what I expected of him. I had not granted him the space to be the only person he could be—himself.

Forgiveness. It's not something you do. It's not something you feel. It's just a way of seeing.

PRACTICE

Copy this excerpt in your Daily Journal.

Do you want peace? Forgiveness offers it. Do you want happiness, a quiet mind, a certainty of purpose, and a sense of worth and beauty that transcends the world? Do you want care and safety, and the warmth of sure protection always? Do you want a quietness that cannot be disturbed, a gentleness that never can be hurt, a deep, abiding comfort, and a rest so perfect it can never be upset? All this forgiveness offers you. You who want peace can find it only by complete forgiveness. In complete forgiveness, in which you recognize that there is nothing to forgive, you are absolved completely.

A Course in Miracles

Look at your writing. With minute care observe the number of jagged *i* dots.

#46

To soften your heart a bit, start by replacing them with simple dots placed directly above the *i* stem.

#47

Look also for loops inside the circle letters: *a, o, d, g,* and *q.*

#48

If they occur more than once or twice, slow down and omit them. The ideal circle letter has no inner loops of any kind.

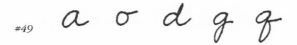

#49

Begin making yours this way. It will give you permission to speak the truth in order to *heal,* not to hurt, justify, or show how smart you are.

If angles predominate in your writing, replace at least half of them with soft garlands.

#50   *Worth   worth*

This will slow down your analytical/critical nature and give you and those around you more space just to be as you are.

If your writing tends to be small and compressed,

#51   *sense of wroth and beauty*

you live in a cozy nest of "shoulds" and can't see over the edge. Spontaneous generosity is not in your nature. You may give gifts, but when you do, you keep track because you find it difficult to let go. To counter this attitude, create an overall openness in your writing pattern.

#52   *sense of worth and beauty*

To do so consistently and purposefully, you will begin to create an expansion of your very spirit. You could call it a "generosity of being."

An essential key to **Forgiveness** is the letter *c,* especially, but not only, the capital *C.* Go back and look at yours. Since there are no capital *C*'s in the paragraph you just wrote, make a few of them for practice to remind you of how yours are shaped.

If there are any initial configurations in this letter, it is an indicator that you have created a powerfully negative link between you and another person; the link is negative judgment. Look at the introductory part of

the letter. Is it a hook,   #53   *C*   a circle,   #54   *C*

or something that drives into the letter creating a deep angle?

#55 *ℓ*

The size and character of the stroke indicate how tightly you are holding on to a past negative experience. Look at the loop as a noose and the hook as a grappling hook. If you write your *C*'s as in the last example, you are still reliving events of the past and you are determined not to let them go. With *C*'s like this, **Forgiveness** is out of reach. If you make any of these strokes and want to be free of harsh judgment, begin to write your letter *C* in this manner:

#56 C C C peace can

Try a few lines of them. See how it feels. Then write words that have *c* in them. This sentence will be good practice:

Carol Corsica claims that cushy cocoons continually cover crazy courses on Charlie Casey's tennis courts.

How did that feel? That slight stroke change alone can shift your tendency toward harsh, opinionated perceptions of past experiences, to holding more thoughtful and compassionate views of them. If you practice consistently until the stroke change flows automatically, you may be amazed at the change it will make in your personal relationships. This is a powerful change to make, especially if you have deep-seated parent issues.

Start changing the unforgiving pattern that occurs most frequently in your writing; then, one at a time, change the others. Do your homework on each stroke for at least three weeks in a row before you go on to the next one. If you work on more than one at a time, your brain will protest and shut down, and you may give up. *One stroke at a time.*

As you practice **Forgiveness** strokes, embrace each one as a long-lost friend reentering your life—a friend who demonstrates ongoing support for you, and cheers you on in achieving your highest purpose in life. By practicing the above changes faithfully, every day without fail, you can transform the quality of every relationship in your life. You can begin to see life as a mirror.

By changing your writing patterns, you are not denying that specific incidents occurred. No changing that. They happened. Nor are you repressing the pain they caused. Clearly, you have every right to suffer. If you have any doubts, open your Daily Journal and write down the name of one person who has brought suffering into your life: a person you feel it is nearly impossible to forgive. Just write their name down. Now list three or four ways or incidents in which she or he has caused suffering in your life. Be brief, specific, and to the point. You might write:

MY MOTHER

1. She never read story books to me or held me in her lap.

2. She wanted a boy and I was a girl.

3. She never listened to me, she just hit me and yelled a lot.

Now reread the list aloud, one item at a time. Absorb the meaning of each item you have listed and how it has shaped you through the years. By now there should be no doubt about it. You are entitled to suffer, you have earned the right to it.

If you really want to be free of negative judgment, transform your suffering into a source of grace and healing. You can see your past through the lens of forgiveness simply by making a choice. Rather than clinging to the right to suffer for the rest of your life, you can choose to give up that right. Just give it up. If you make that choice, incorporating these simple writing changes will support your intentions. You are choosing to release negative judgment. You are choosing to let go of the right to suffer. You are choosing to be free.

CHAPTER SEVEN

Fluidity of Thought

A fluid mind contains many thoughts

without clutching possessively

at any of them.

· Anonymous ·

DECLARATION TO MY WHOLENESS

My heart welcomes Truth

in its many disguises.

FLUIDITY IS A FLOW sloshing back and forth gently and shape-lessly, moving in harmonious, graceful action. When we speak of fluid thinkers, we picture those who can entertain opposing ideas with a certain brightness and lack of judgment. We imagine that those thinkers have a sense of curiosity and inquiry rather than intellectual rectitude. Fluid thinking allows one to play with concepts rather than to work with them. Ease and the ability to cope in stressful situations are basic characteristics of the fluid thinker.

Most of us picture ourselves to be flexible in thought and to be at least fairly fluid thinkers. Here's a simple test to find out if you are fooling yourself. Reflect for a moment and be honest when you answer these three simple questions.

1. Do you have many opinions?

2. When you listen to ideas that oppose yours, do you have an immediate retort to back up what *you* think?

3. When someone expresses ideas that are contrary to your own, is your original viewpoint carefully intact after a discussion with them?

If you answered yes to any of these questions, and then justified your responses, you may be a little less fluid in your thinking than others may think you are!

All three questions are focused around holding opinions, which is in direct opposition to thinking fluidly. Opinions can be killers. They deaden inquiry. They build an impenetrable wall around the heart, obliterating the light. They rigorously protect themselves from the intrusion of outsiders. They strangle the Truth, withholding all the breath from it. Do you really want to discover the Truth in life? Simply let go of your most cherished opinions!

Try this experiment for one week. Every time you begin to say the words "should," "I think," or "I believe," STOP! Check yourself and don't let those words take form. Either be quiet or reshape what you were going to say without using those phrases. "You might want to consider" is an excellent substitute phrase. It creates an opening for opposing ideas to flow in. Give it a try, just for one week. You may learn something about yourself. And as you're practicing getting out of your own way, be sure to incorporate the writing changes below. Fluidity of thought. A quantum step toward freedom!

PRACTICE

Copy this paragraph in your Daily Journal.

> *The only reason someone is a genius, and knows things you do not know, is because he has opened his mind to contemplate the what-ifs, the outrageous thoughts, the thoughts of brilliance that go beyond the limited thinking of man. He has allowed himself to entertain and reason with these thoughts, whereas you have rejected them.*

> *Ramtha*

Look at your *th*. Does it flow into a ligature? This is a ligature.

#57   *th*

A ligature was quite common until the nineteenth century, but is now considered unusual since it is not in any copy books. It is a method of using part of one letter to connect it with the one that follows. The *th* ligature is the most common. If your *th* is not a ligature, pick up your pen and write a few of them, similar to the one above. Make sure you do not let the crossbar create a bowl-like shape.

#58   *Xh*

This shape will divert your energy from setting a meaningful goal. The *t* crossbar is your willpower stroke. When it curves deeply, your will is being diverted in some way. Your plans will slosh around inside the bowl and will lack drive and direction. Be very sure to keep that crossbar high. The placement indicates how far you are willing to stretch to reach your goals, and how high you are willing to set them to begin with.

The following is an excellent practice sentence to write when you are playing with ligatures:

Then the thicket thinned though the thistles threatened through the thick leather thongs.

Write this a few times using the *th* ligature, being careful that it drives upward and does not become a bowl crossbar. How does it feel?

If you already have this ligature in your writing , experiment with yet another stroke. This is what is called the *figure-eight g.*

#59   *ƒ g genius*

This is not only the symbol of very fluid thinkers but also of those who bring immense individuality into their profession: creative writers, public speakers, and those people who live, breathe, and consider their profession their *life*, not just something they *do*. Because of their mental fluidity, these writers often philosophize without getting stuck in a particular belief system, and they have the ability to be dramatically creative. When you see the figure-eight *g*, think of "*g* for gold," for it is as precious an element in handwriting as the metal is from the earth. Be certain as you make them that the finishing stroke goes all the way up to the baseline. If you tend to have a tight script—one in which there is a pattern of rigidity and sameness, especially if all the letters within the words are connected—

#60 *genius*

begin to replace your regular *g*'s with the figure-eight *g*.

#61 *genius*

It will soften your critical edges, begin to pry you loose from fear, and add a lightness to your heart.

For about a week, write slowly when you use your notebook, replacing only a few *g*'s with the figure-eight *g*. As you are able to go a little faster, replace more of them. By the end of three weeks of practice, convert at least 90 percent of them to the figure-eight *g*. Be rigorous in your practice, and watch areas of your life transform. Your creative juices will begin to flow in unusual ways and your thought patterns may surprise you in their ability to be flexible. Go for the gold!

CHAPTER EIGHT

Patience

We have what we seek.

It is there all the time,

and if we give it time

it will make itself known to us.

· Thomas Merton ·

DECLARATION TO MY WHOLENESS

The timing of my life is in God's hands.

I accept it as perfect for me.

P ATIENCE IS NOT an easy quality for most of us. We set our goals, create the strategy to achieve them, do our part in order to accomplish them, and when the expected results do not spring forth in the time frame we had set, we have one of several reactions. **1. Blame.** They (or I) did something wrong **2. Question.** What did they (or I) do wrong? **3. Introspect.** Something's trying to happen here. Please show me the lesson.

Like most qualities, **Patience** does not exist autonomously inside of us. Without **Trust** it is immobilized and cannot function. Not forceful or manipulative, not determined and wresting, **Patience** is not only the willingness to wait for an outcome, it is also having a sense of wonder and delight at what the outcome will be. **Patience** teaches us to be kind, especially to ourselves. It teaches us to banish blame from our lives and replace it with a sense of wonder at our individual participation in the Great Scheme of Things. It teaches us to look at our mistakes as timely occurrences, stumbling blocks that we are polishing into stepping stones. **Patience** shows us that waiting has its benefits—often great advantages. **Patience** is acknowledging (without having to understand) that everything is working out exactly as it is supposed to, and honoring each step in the unfolding process.

PRACTICE

Copy this paragraph in your Daily Journal.

You've got to go at the rate you can go. You wake up at the rate you wake up. You're finished with your desires at the rate you finish with your desires. The disequilibrium comes into harmony at the rate it comes into harmony. You can't rip the skin off the snake. The snake must moult the skin.

Ram Dass

Hold your paper away from you and pay special attention to several things: the slant, angles, or loops in the Lower Zone, and strokes that look like this:

#62

Does your slant seem to lean far to the right?

#63 *desires*

If it slants this far to the right, or even more, you might want to pull it up a bit to be more vertical. The more rightward the slant, the more emotionally reactive you can be, and the less patient you are with waiting. You want it now, especially if the pen exerts enough pressure to create an indentation on the page. If your writing leans severely forward, you tend to get caught up in the drama of what's going on without slowing down and reflecting on possible outcomes. **Patience**. The more vertical the writing, the more clear-thinking and objective the writer. Do not overcorrect, however, to the point that your handwriting has a back slant.

#64 *desires*

A back slant (which has nothing to do with being right or left-handed, by the way) is a demonstration of withdrawing your radiance from your environment. Oh, you may be outgoing and talk a mile a minute, but the real you does not stand up to be counted. For whatever reasons from your past, you perceive it as unsafe to express your real dreams, hopes, and visions. If you doubt this, begin writing absolutely vertical for a few days and see what it feels like. The words that come up most frequently among my clients are "threatening" and "scary." Just try it and see what it does for you. The easiest way to practice writing vertically is to purchase lined binder paper and turn it sideways, then keep the slant aligned with the lines on the paper.

#65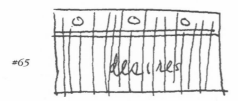

Now let's get back to your Lower Zone. (See page 140 for a description of zones.) What does it look like? A mass of loops? If so, are they slender, or large and full of movement? Do they head off to the right or to the left? None at all? How long are your *descenders*? (A descender is the line that drives into the Lower Zone to create the loop.)

#66

Either extreme—exceedingly short or exceedingly long and active descenders—can be a sign of impatience.

Remember: One stroke by itself provides only a part of the picture. Keep in mind the One Grand Question of handwriting analysis when you see one stroke that you know the meaning of: This stroke is *in relation to what?* Always . . . *in relation to what?* For example, if you find very short descenders

#67   U   q

combined with heavy writing and omitted *i* dots, *t* crossbars,

#68   *with*

and perhaps even omitted words, you are filled with anxiety to get to the goal by the shortest route possible. You tend to be short-cut oriented, and often miss the subtle details involved in the process.

Impatience is also shown by heavily drawn loops that are excessively large, especially when they tangle with the line below. "Let's just get there!" is what they shout. If you have larger than usual lower loops and you tend to write through them in the next line,

#69   *you wake up finished with*

rather than reduce the size of the loop, begin to avoid writing through them.

This will enable you to slow down and sort through the components of your life and prioritize more carefully. If your writing is heavily drawn and consistently cuts through lower loops, you have so many things going on in your life that the ability to prioritize has all but vanished. Slow down! Breathe! Take it easy on yourself! As you begin to untangle your writing you will also begin untangling your life.

Another descender to watch for looks something like this:

#70 q 4 4p

It will vary a bit with the writer, but it can occur in any letter that normally goes below the baseline. As you can see, there is no loop, only a Lower Zone pull-away stroke. The precise significance is determined by which letter it occurs in, but in any Lower Zone letter it is a sign of aggression, which can be either positive or negative. When this stroke is combined with a far rightward slant, *control strokes,* and missing or carelessly placed *i* dots and *t* stems, the writer will plant seeds, keep pulling up the roots of the seedling to see how it's doing, shake it vigorously and snap, "Will you just *hurry up!* When will you ever bear fruit! I want it now!" **Patience**. Accept the timing. Honor the process.

Another stroke pattern to be aware of is the *arcade*.

#71 m n h

Paternal and protective, their very form tells about their nature. By themselves they are not indicative of control, but in combination with exceedingly short descenders, jagged *i* dots, and down-sloping crossbars, however, they indicate a writer who hovers over their environment in a controlling fashion.

#72 *into harmony*

Control strokes of any kind will paralyze your efforts toward **Patience**. They can occur in any letter, but are most common in the *t* crossbar, *i* dots, and printed capital letters. They look like this:

#73

Look at the paragraph you have written. Do you see regularly occurring control strokes? If so, and especially if they're heavily drawn, and if they occur in more than one letter, and give the appearance of slashes on the paper, you have a need to be in control. Others may see you as having the tendency to dominate people or situations.

If these strokes appear consistently in your writing, yet you consider yourself a patient person, you may want to look again and see if what you call "patience" has to do with how tightly you hold the reins. If you are willing to loosen them a bit as a way of experimenting, try any of the suggested writing changes in this section. Practice them consistently for three weeks, don't give up (patience! patience!), and you may even find your blood pressure going down. Above all, enjoy the process.

There is a stress-reduction exercise you may want to try when you are feeling squeezed-in by life. It is simple to do and may reduce your anxiety and blood pressure. Called Miles of Lace, it looks like this:

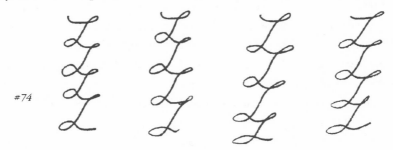

#74

When you decorate a page gently with these strokes for a few minutes, you will find yourself breathing more deeply, and your whole body will relax. Pick up your pen and write a few lines—or fill a page—right now. See how it feels. Do this exercise anytime you need to slow down your energy, and it can put you right back in your center.

Another stress-reduction writing stroke is called the *propeller stroke*. It looks like this:

#75 — *ffffff*

Write lines of this particular exercise only when you need to slow down and reverse forward-moving energy, either physical or emotional. Whatever you do, **do not incorporate this stroke into your daily writing**, especially in the lower loop of the letter *f.* This is very important. When written as the lower loop in the *f,* it is called a *self-sabotage stroke* because its reverse energy flow in the Lower Zone (project orientation and relationships) causes you to resist firm commitment and forward motion. If the propeller stroke occurs in your writing consistently, know that when you tend to get right up to the point where you will succeed, something happens to cause you to fail. When you get to the moment of commitment, you walk away.

The propeller stroke is very subtle because it weaves a thread of reverse energy into your life. It is best used situationally as a therapeutic exercise to slow down forward-moving emotions and turn them around.

If you want to experience directly the effects of Miles of Lace or the propeller stroke, try this. The next time you place a phone call that requires an immediate and straightforward answer from the party you are calling and you keep being put on "hold," draw line after line of propellers and lace as you are waiting, and see how you feel. Use a colored pen if one is handy, to lighten your mood. If you have time to draw many lines, you may start to feel so calm and centered that when your call is finally put through, you may ask *them* to hold for a moment while you finish drawing that last line.

CHAPTER NINE

Willingness To Risk

What would you attempt to do

if you knew you could not fail?

· Robert Schuller ·

DECLARATION TO MY WHOLENESS

In perfect faith and open to miracles,

I embrace the unexpected.

AS THE CONSCIOUSNESS of the world shifts on all levels, security as we have known it is transforming dramatically. It no longer has the significance it did twenty, fifteen, or five years ago, or even last week, for that matter. The institutions we used to rely upon to take care of us are being de-mythicized and reshaped: the once invincible Soviet Union, church representatives, savings and loans, the physician as healer, job security—the list goes on and on.

As traditions tumble down, we are being challenged to shape our own ways of seeing, believing, and relating. With fewer institutional walls to lean against, we are being called upon to reach deep inside ourselves to the *common core of knowing* that unites all human beings. We are being invited to stand upon our own two feet and create ways of interacting that not only support each of us individually, but also our planetary family. For the first time in history, we are being given the opportunity to create a world that works for every sentient being as well as for the environment around us: a world of cooperation not competition; principle-centered leadership; win-win situations; peace rather than war to support the economy—all interdependent concepts that support life.

To be effective in carrying through with these ideals, we cannot rely on historic patterns; there are none. We are being called upon to invent our own. This involves the absolute necessity of having a **Willingness to Risk**. Inventing! Creating! Doing what's never been done! Stepping into areas where we have never been and doing what we have only dreamed of, with no prototype to imitate and only our imagination with which to draw the map. This is scary only because we've never been there, but what an exciting and worthwhile path to pursue.

PRACTICE

Copy this paragraph in your Daily Journal.

> *To cling to the familiar, we will pay almost any price. An extreme example is the story my great-grandmother used to tell of a woman whose husband beat her regularly. When asked why she didn't leave the man, the woman replied, "I can't leave. I don't know what I would do out there." This woman was unwilling to risk going "out there" for fear that it would be worse than where she was. To one degree or another, we all do this, over and over again. . . . We call this unwillingness to risk "security." To transcend fear you must be willing to risk. You must be willing to go beyond your comfort zone.*
>
> *Terry Cole-Whittaker*

While keeping your notebook open to the paragraph you have just written, hold the paper away from you. If your writing looks compressed, open it up! A visual image to keep in mind when you think "compressed" or "opened up" is an accordion. When it is squeezed shut, there is no possibility of sound. When it is expanded, breath is expressed and musical notes can be played.

#76

security   *security*

As you open up your letters, you will begin to shape your life less and less according to someone else's plan and begin to live openly in your own uniqueness. You will give yourself permission to write your own music and interpret life's musical score as *you* hear it.

Line direction? Be an optimist! Either have your line go straight across the page with a consistent baseline or slightly upward.

#77

If it starts to slant downward, alter your line so that it doesn't.

#78

The margin is a major factor in the **Willingness to Risk**. If you hug the left side of the page when you write, you tend to lean on the past for security and answers.

#79

Those feelings will not disappear with the shift in the margin, but when you consistently create a left margin of ¾ to 1 inch, you will begin to view them with more distance: as memories rather than how-to-live reference books. Experiment to see how it feels! If there is resistance, you know that you're on the right track. **Remember Noble Truth #4:** *The greater the difficulty, the greater the value.*

The next stroke is last only because it is the most difficult to change in this trait cluster. It is called a *retraced downstroke in the Mid Zone*. I mention it in regard to several qualities in this book because it is so negatively powerful. You don't want to write them. Not ever. Vacuumlike, they suck us into the past and have us repeating patterns established *for* us but not *by* us. They are based on fear: of being different; of not being understood; of not complying; of not being liked; and, above all, the fear of being left alone . . . all alone. Of all the traits mentioned in this section, retraced downstrokes in the Mid Zone *are the most significant*.

A retraced downstroke is just what it sounds like: a stroke that first goes down to the baseline, then as the pen moves upward from the baseline it retraces the stroke that just went down.

#80

All elementary-school penmanship books have this stroke in the *m, n, h,* and *k.* (See page 138.) These retraced downstrokes are exceedingly supressive to creative thinking . . . that's why unusually creative children often agonize over their handwriting in school. They cannot follow the crowd! Not only do they resist coloring inside the lines, they either want to draw their own lines, or they don't want lines at all!

Look at the paragraph you have just finished writing. Are there consistent retraces? If so, try this:

#81

This is called a pull-away stroke because that is exactly what you are affirming when you draw it. You are daring to pull away from what you have been told in the past and moving into how *you* say it shall be.

you have been told in the past and moving into how *you* say it shall be. If that is an uncommon experience for you, writing this particular stroke may be a struggle, but what a victory once you have mastered it! Practice it letter after letter, line after line, week after week. The **Willingness to Risk** will breathe life into the very essence of your Self and express that Self openly the way only you can.

If you have dreams and are exceedingly frustrated because they have not been manifested, but you are willing to do whatever it takes to see them come to life, incorporate all of the above strokes in your writing, *one stroke for three weeks at a time.* Remember to date your notebook pages. Truly, miracles will begin to abound in every area of your life as these strokes begin to flow automatically and feel natural to you. **Willingness to Risk** is letting go of the trunk and getting out on the skinny branches of life!

Once these pull-aways become natural for you, and they are comfortably integrated into your writing, you will assume a new posture when chaos tempts you to withdraw into old patterns. First, vigorously write several lines of words with pull-aways in them, then put your pen down and do this exercise: Close your eyes so you can't see, put your hands over your ears so you can't hear, and imagine that you are mute . . . then mentally repeat this declaration again and again: "Life is either a daring adventure or it is nothing." Who first uttered these words? Helen Keller.

CHAPTER TEN

Being Here, Now

You can learn from the past,

you can plan for the future,

but it is only in the present

that you can act.

· Jeffrey Wildfogel ·

DECLARATION TO MY WHOLENESS

I honor the past and put it lovingly

behind me. I leave the future to God.

I am the creator of my own life:

right here, right now.

SOUNDS EASY. Being present right now. But how often do we practice it? Our minds are constantly reviewing our unchangeable yesterdays in order to create our theoretical tomorrows. And where does that leave us? Certainly not in the present! Firmly entrenched anywhere but in the here and now, our mind dwells on the following thoughts: "If I had only... ," "Why did I ... ," "I wish I hadn't ... ," "Tomorrow I'll ... ," "She/he had no right to ...." Gradually, we begin to shape a box around us that we call *My Life*, with shame, guilt, regret, and blame as the four supporting sides. As we predictably repeat our past habits and attitudes and things begin to appear bleak and hopeless, we reach up for the lid called *That's Just How It Is!* and pull it down over our head. Then we have the cheek to call our experiences *Life*.

Just do this for a moment: pretend that you have just been created. As you are. All grown up. Right where you are right now. You have no past, no memories, and there is no such thing as the future because you haven't invented it yet. The whole world is open to you. Since you just got here you know no one and no one has any opinions about who you are, what you should be doing, or how you should be doing it. Your life is yours to create in your own way. That's it. Now close your eyes. This is your world. Be fully present only to exactly where you are. Now decide who you are according to what *you* say. Dream it. Imagine it wildly. Pull out all the stops. Paint it with blazing colors! Remember, no one else exists, so there is no "they" to worry about, as in "What will *they* think?" You've never been anywhere or done anything. You are right here, right now.

PRACTICE

In your Daily Journal, describe who you are and what you want to do. Write at least two full, fat paragraphs, but don't stop there if you're really having fun!

Being Here, Now. Look at what you've just written to see if you have any of the following writing patterns, singly or in combination:

Inexact placement or lack of *i* dots or *t* crossbars

#82

Little or no left margin

#83

Backlash strokes

#84

Compressed writing

#85

Lower Zone loops that underscore letters to the left

#86

If more than one of these characteristics is present in your writing you may rest assured that you have arranged your memory in such a way that you not only *refer* to the past for answers, you *stand in it* and shout to the present, dictating how your life shall be. As a result, the past is on a continual loop as it plays out in your life.

Look at your *i* dots. Where do you place them? High and off to the right?

#87   ✓

Or high and off to the left?

#88   ✓

Not so high but off to either right or left?

#89   ✓   ✓

No *i* dots at all?

#90   ✓

If you want to be here, now, and attentive to who you are being and what you are doing at this moment, dot each *i* with a simple dot placed directly over the *i* stem.

#91   *i i i*

Do not use a circle or jagged formation or slash. Use only a dot.

Check out your left margin. If your writing begins close to the edge of the paper, creating only a scanty margin, move it out at least 1 inch from the left edge of the page.

#92

If you have consistently created a slender margin for any length of time, this change may feel as though someone is looking over your shoulder or wagging a scolding finger in your face. Not to worry. It's just the past.

Now look at your stroke endings. Do any of them end up directed back to the left? Remember, the left represents the past. (See #79.) When these occur at the end of words they are called backlash strokes . . . and for good reason. *The American Heritage Dictionary* defines *backlash* as "an antagonistic reaction to some prior action construed as a threat." If you want to stop blaming the past for your lot in life and begin accepting the freedom of being responsible for your own life, end all of your strokes to the right. If you make what is called the *delta d,*

#93

begin it at the top, swinging down to create the circle, and end it in a rightward direction.

To those left-handers who say that they end some strokes to the left because of their particular handedness, I give you my word, that is not why you do it. It has to do with thought patterns and not handedness patterns. *How you see life* moves that pen. Look carefully at your *t* cross-bars to make sure that they go from left to right.

#94

If they don't, gradually begin to change them so that they do.

Compressed writing is exactly what it sounds like. It is a sign of being stuck in the past with the inability to be spontaneous and open to the present moment. I mention compressed writing again and again because it puts the brakes on our creativity. Remember the accordion example in **Willingness To Risk**.

Just looking at compressed writing tells you that there is not much breathing going on. If your writing resembles this, open it up. Spread it out! Give yourself air. Inhale deeply. When you begin to experience resistance, know that it isn't the pen or your fingers that are resisting, or an aversion to "how funny it looks." It is your past dictating your present by quoting from your past history and insisting you take notes. Resist! Resist! Resist! And open up your writing! You can create only when you are standing in the present. **Be Here, Now!**

I have said it before and I will say it again: Begin only one of these changes for a period of three weeks at a time before you go on to the next change. Practice them in your notebook daily before you attempt to integrate them into your regular writing. You're not dealing with just pen pushing here. You are working on deeply ingrained habits of thinking. Be patient and resolute. This is power-packed technology and it works. **Remember Noble Truth # 4**: *The degree of difficulty in the mastery of a stroke change is directly proportional to the value it will have in your life.*

CHAPTER ELEVEN

Friendship

The world is round so that

friendship may circle it.

· Pierre Teilhard de Chardin ·

DECLARATION TO MY WHOLENESS

I am an honest, trustworthy confidant

to all who call me friend.

WHEN I FIRST BEGAN teaching, I shared information that I had learned from books. It was valid information, but not always the outgrowth of personal experience. As a result, much of what I taught remained on the intellectual level, the outer knowing level. Once I realized that truth is not what you know, but what you have experienced, my focus shifted. (See **Forgiveness**.) Although much has been written about **Friendship** through the ages in the most sublime and eloquent terms, I have made a conscious choice not to quote them here because **Friendship** is a weaving not of minds, but of hearts. Please hold my hand as we go on. Thank you.

I am blessed with a few rare friends in my life who love me. Some of these friends are my children; some are not. In our friendships there are no strings attached. No expectations. They just love me and I just love them. I didn't say we understand one another. Oh no. In fact we are all so different that at times we just need breathing space to be apart. And even then, we just love each other.

When we have deep inner sharings that must get out, we call one another or meet for tea or go for a hike. Even with all of the intimate stories we have shared, none of us has ever made the other feel different, crazy, or the least bit unusual. We are just who we are, being who we are, completely. We know our hearts are safe with one another. We listen clearly with neither advice nor criticism to offer. We accept one another just as we are, and unless we sense an openness, or receive a direct request such as, "Please tell me what you see," we don't suggest changes. We never lie to each other and we don't flatter. We never speak negatively about one another to anyone else, even when we're upset. If we do something that the other feels is out of line, we mention it, never with blame, but rather with honest, direct feedback without any value judgment. It may sting for a moment, but that happens only when we take it personally. Our shared observations are never personal because we address what the other person has *done*, not who they *are*.

From the receiving end, I can say that my friends dive through my imperfections all the way into my heart and love me for being the only person I know how to be—me. We laugh together at the dumb things in ourselves, and they never judge me or tell me how I should be. Not ever.

When we hurt, the other feels the pain, but we never try to take it away as though it shouldn't be. We listen. We support. Sometimes we cry together. We wipe away the tears. We also draw clear boundaries. We honor the path the other must follow, knowing that although we're all headed toward the same destination, we may have chosen different paths to get there.

We also laugh together a lot. We can be silly. Sometimes we have fun and sometimes we are cross. We give each other special little things for no reason at all: a stone from the beach or an especially beautiful pine cone; maybe a rubber stamp or a picture postcard; or a discarded skin that some snake slipped out of on a rocky hillside. They often find extraordinary handwriting samples for me, wrap them up, and send them to me in the mail. Or they write me a note with their nondominant hand, and then draw a picture to go with it. We give gifts that touch the other in a significant way. We are always there for one another with a hug, a shoulder to cry on, a heart to listen, and kindness—above all, kindness. We experience the sacredness of true friendship yet have no need to put it in words. We know what it feels like to be wealthy, to be okay, and to be loved.

PRACTICE

Copy these few paragraphs in your Daily Journal.

> *When I was 10 years old, one of my best friends was 80, and his name was Mr. Boggs. He called me his "twirly friend" (because I did a wheely in his driveway). Mr. Boggs taught me how to play checkers and gave me a microscope. Then he got sick and went into the hospital. Every day I made him a card or a poem or did a drawing and sent these to the hospital. Mr. Boggs came home after a month in the hospital and said to me, "You saved my life. No one else called or wrote, and your mailings gave me the courage to live. Thank you."*

> *SARK*

The willingness to give and the willingness to receive. Generosity of Spirit. Knowing what to overlook. Kindness coupled with honesty. All of this is apparent in **Friendship** . . . and in handwriting. Look at the paragraph you just copied, noting particularly the cramped or open appearance of the writing. If your letters look compressed (remember the accordion) practice opening them up. Pay special attention to your communication letters: *a, o, d, g,* and *q.* Make very sure that they don't have inner loops. Just as a reminder, these are inner loops.

#95 *a a o o d g q*

Do your very best not to make them. Wherever you see inner loops, write slowly and remove them, making each communication letter gently full and uncluttered.

#96   *a   o   d   g   g*

If you continue to find inner loops, write this sentence in your journal:

Pippin apples, pink grapefruit, plump oranges, oblong pears, and ripe bananas go together to make an organically sumptuous salad.

Check your circle letters for clarity, then look at the letter *p*. Is there a pull-away stroke below the baseline?

#97   *p*

This can be a sign of aggression, which has both its positive and negative aspects. If you have this stroke, don't make yourself wrong for having it, but if it occurs regularly *and* your letters or words are cramped *and* your writing tends to be more angular than soft in appearance, you might want to focus on writing your *p* in a different way.

First, do this: Draw your stroke down into the Lower Zone, then trace right back up over it. Come to the baseline, draw a round full circle, then release the stroke at the baseline carrying it off to the right.

#98   *p*

Or, if you prefer, do a print-script *p* instead of writing one.

#99   *P*

This will take you off the defensive and allow you to take a deep breath before you move into action.

If you want to bring a little lightheartedness into your life and be known as someone anyone can talk to, begin practicing the above stroke patterns every day. As they become more and more automatic, be on the lookout for initial hooks on any stroke, but especially on the *t* crossbar.

#100   𝓉

Make a conscious effort to eliminate these hooks. A hook does exactly what it sounds like. On the *t* crossbar, the willpower stroke, you are hooked into having your own way, and you hold fast to your own ideas. There is nothing wrong with that, but if you have the aggressive stroke in your *p*, your natural writing tends to be compressed, your script tends to be angular, and you have initial hooks in your *t* crossbar, you are not only hooked into having your own way, you are invested in it!

Friendship is also the ability to laugh with someone and see the lighter side without the need to be right. After you have mastered the above changes, you might want to add a *humor flourish* or a *friendship flourish*. A humor flourish looks like this:

#101   𝓂

A friendship flourish looks like this:

#102   𝓜   𝓝   𝓐

Example #101 is most commonly used as an introductory stroke into the capital *M* or *N*. Example #102 is used not only for the *M* and *N*, but also to create the capital *A*. Pick up your pen and give them a try.

Make a few lines of capital *M*'s, something like this, noting how the arcades slope gently downward and the final stroke dances off in a gracious motion at the baseline.

#103

This pattern reaffirms your ability to listen without judgment and speak without fear. Written in this manner it is called the *letter of grace*. No need to be right. No need to criticize. Just a gentle flow of energy, reaching out to life.

Now write a few lines of lower case *n*'s. If you have a real resistance to writing them this way, do a few more lines of them. Notice how you feel as you write them. Do a few more. Does it make you feel like dancing?

Using examples #101 and #102 as models, write a line or two of capital *M*'s, *N*'s and *A*'s. How does it feel? Combined with the other changes above, once these strokes becomes automatic and flow across the page effortlessly, people around you will wonder what put you in such a good mood! I have had many clients tell me that once these particular writing changes became automatic, the question they were asked most frequently was, "Are you in love?" **Friendship:** A mirror of Self.

CHAPTER TWELVE

Simplicity

Be as simple as you can be;

you will be astonished to see how

uncomplicated and happy

your life can become.

· Paramhansa Yogananda ·

DECLARATION TO MY WHOLENESS

My life is abundant and

my needs are few.

I USED TO EQUATE **Simplicity** with Poverty, and from that belief I voluntarily courted them both and embraced the latter. I felt that owning next to nothing would make me holy, closer to God, and that I would experience a sense of freedom from the material world. Odd. It had quite the opposite effect. Once I had almost no material possessions, most of my attention was taken up with acquiring what I needed for bare day-to-day survival! Rather than simplifying my life, poverty complicated it terribly. It took me years to see that self-inflicted poverty is brash and painful and has everything to do with escaping, but nothing to do with **Simplicity**. **Simplicity** is elegant and wise, and whispers with dignity. It is the silent midpoint between having too much and having too little.

From that difficult, long-term relationship with poverty, I came to learn that what I sought was not really poverty, but balance. **Simplicity** was my teacher. She taught me that I didn't have to do away with material possessions in order to live a simple life, but rather to reprioritize my values. I learned to ask different questions. Rather than asking, "How do I get what I need?" I stood in square one and asked, "Am I here for a reason? What is my life all about anyway? Who am I? How do I create a vision for my life?" I infused these questions with the intensity of a burning commitment *to know*. Commitment backed up by strong willpower generates answers from the most unusual and unimaginable quarters. One by one they came to me. **Simplicity** rearranges your priorities in life by eliminating anything that does not serve your highest purpose.

PRACTICE

Copy this paragraph in your Daily Journal.

> *Living in simplicity is a way toward sharing, joining, and communion with others. Simple living is a kind of fasting. The less I have, the less I have to take care of; the less time I have to spend caring for and protecting it; and the more time and energy I have to share with God and with others. In addition, I contribute to the ecology of the earth itself; this illustrates yet again that when I heal myself, everyone and everything, even the earth itself, is healed as well.*

> *Peggy Tabor Millin*

A quick glance at the paragraph you have just written will give you a clear indication of the presence or absence of **Simplicity** in your life. How ornate or frilly is your writing? Is one zone or stroke pattern more exaggerated than others and out of balance?

#104

Living   *Living*

Living

Simplicity by its very definition implies "balance"—not too much and not too little. If you have ascenders towering up into the Upper Zone that are about three times the size of the Mid Zone,

#105 *fasting*

you might want to shorten them just a bit. Two- to two-and-a-half times the size of the Mid Zone is considered an ideally balanced Upper Zone.

#106 *fasting*

If, however, your Upper Zone is almost nonexistent and most of the letters stay right in the Mid Zone,

#107 *fasting*

you might be overemphasizing issues such as the following: "Am I wearing the right clothes? Does my hair look okay? Did I say the right thing? Does she like me?" If this is the case, I strongly recommend that you stretch your ascenders upward to the ideal height and create a gentle Lower Zone. Balance reduces stress.

Does your writing tend to be bottom heavy with excess activity in the Lower Zone?

#108 *fasting*

Is it the first thing that catches your eye when you look at the sheet of paper? Here are a few loops to imitate if your Lower Zone is out of control.

#109 *f g y j z*

They will reinforce your ability to draw simple boundaries instead of agonizing over your relationships. This gentle loop adjustment can greatly simplify your life.

Simplicity also involves speech. Talking less and conserving words is an heart-opening discipline. If any of your communication letters—*a, o, d, g,* or *q*—are consistently open at the top, gently close them.

#110 *a o d g q*

a o d g q

This will support your efforts to speak less. If you detect hooks at the beginning of words,

#111 *ecology of the earth*

you might consider eliminating them. This type of hook reflects the sense that one's security lies in material possessions.

The modification of the shape of the *l* and *h* loops is a compatible change that easily accompanies the closure of the top of any communication letter and the elimination of the initial hook in letters. Extend your *l*'s and *h*'s to be two and a half times the height of the Mid Zone, and create a moderate loop in each.

#112 *healed*

By keeping your *l* and *h* tall, you will become more and more open to your essential spiritual nature and find yourself automatically going to your higher Self rather than to your ego self for answers. Remember to create the arcade in the *h* by consciously avoiding retracing the down-stroke. Create a pull-away stroke instead.

#113

When we studied ancient history in school, most of us learned that the inscription over the gateway to the temple at Delphi was Know Thyself. What most of us did not learn is that there was yet a second row of print beneath the first, consisting of three simple words: Nothing in Excess. If any phrase could sum up the perfect meaning of **Simplicity**, that is it.

CHAPTER THIRTEEN

Resentment

Resentment choreographs a

danse macabre for creativity,

aliveness, and joy.

· Anonymous ·

DECLARATION TO MY WHOLENESS

Free from resentment and blame,

I embrace every part of my life

with a joyful heart.

I INCLUDE THIS ONE negative quality because it is the taproot of that poisonous tree in the middle of our Garden on which righteousness, blame, shame, guilt, regret and joylessness bud, bloom, flourish, and then drop their dead leaves. Our mind says we have a right to these attitudes, yet our heart is pummeled and bloodied by them. They keep us reliving the past and cause us to be utterly powerless to create a present filled with Joy and Aliveness. Only after we remove the root of this noxious tree will its poison fruit cease to flourish.

Ah, but how we clasp this negative emotion to our bosom! With a possessive embrace we cry, "I have a right to be resentful." We stand in the past blaming it and its cast of characters for our present circumstances or attitudes. We let **Resentment** guide us through life, dictating how we shall judge present-day circumstances and people. We abandon to this very expensive emotion our right to choose freely. Expensive? You be the judge. It can cost us a joyful heart, peace of mind, and a sense of fulfillment in relationships—not only with others but with ourselves. It prevents us from living in the present, and causes us to continually repeat old patterns each time we make our choices. Not much personal power there. And certainly no space for transformation. Joy? Out of the question!

PRACTICE

Copy this paragraph in your Daily Journal.

> *As long as you harbor resentment, it is literally impossible for you to picture yourself as a self-reliant, independent, self-determining person who is the Captain of his soul, the master of his Fate. The resentful person turns over his reins to other people. They are allowed to dictate how he shall feel, how he shall act . . . . Resentment is therefore inconsistent with creative goal-striving. In creative goal-striving, you are the actor, not the passive recipient. You set your goals. No one owes you anything . . . . You become responsible for your own success and happiness. Resentment doesn't fit into this picture.*
>
> *Maxwell Maltz*

As you look at your writing, do you notice any strokes beginning beneath the baseline?

#114   *resentment*

The surest way to tell is to hold a piece of paper, ruler, or other straightedge right at the baseline, covering all Mid and Upper Zone letters. Any strokes that start beneath the baseline become obvious. They must be straight, rigid, and inflexible to reflect resentment. These are called *springboard strokes*.

Note the pressure exerted by the pen. Is it heavy or light? Pressure indicates depth of emotion and the length of time we hold on to old memories. Maybe there is even a little hook where you began the below-the-baseline stroke?

#115   *resentment*

That harmless little addition says by definition what it represents: You are hooked into your **Resentment** and are not about to let go of it.

The pressure exerted on the pen and the stiffness of the stroke will say something about the firmness of your stance. The zone in which a stroke begins indicates where the attitude comes from. The zone in which it ends up tells you where it is released. The springboard always begins below the baseline, where past emotional experiences reside. It can be released in either the Upper Zone,

#116   *tment*

which indicates that it remains in the mind and imagination, or it can be released in the Mid Zone,

#117   *resen*

which lets you know right away that you are bringing this attitude into your daily life.

Although a resentful person can be free of this stroke, their resentment will show up in other writing patterns. Be assured, however, that a writer *with* this stroke has a ready reserve of **Resentment**. Coming as it does from the past, **Resentment** is stoked by a memory filled with perceived injustices or emotional injuries that the mind refuses to release. We cling to those memories in order to justify our negative feelings and judgments.

If you find springboards in your handwriting, consciously start the introductory stroke on the baseline using a soft curve.

#118 *resentment*

This is a modified garland, and it will bring a degree of softness into your writing and your heart.

Attitudes that are reflected by springboard strokes are fed from our memory. I have found that the least reliable place to go when I want an honest, unbiased answer is my memory. Most of us bow to it as a holy receptacle of Truth and worship it as a means of justifying our attitudes and behavior, although we reshape, distort, and rearrange it at our own convenience.

Take a walk into your memory for a moment. Be acutely observant as you look around at past happenings and notice that you may have arranged everything in such a way that *you* always had a reason for your decisions and actions. The *other person* was stupid, thoughtless, control-ling, cruel, selfish, etc.—not just once or twice, but every single time. Pretty interesting, isn't it? Funny how we sing praises to our memory by using such phrases as "Well, *I* remember… ," "He *always*…," or "She *never*…," and thereby give ourselves the right to harbor resentment and its entourage of "justifiable" negative emotions. All we are really getting is a fictionalized history that depicts us as the hero, heroine, or martyr.

Take a deep breath, and let's invent a little objectivity for this next exercise. Bring to mind an incident that you are still deeply annoyed about, one about which you say you have a right to be angry or upset. Now close your eyes and take a moment to relive it. See yourself and the other person or persons, in action once again and recall the dialogue as it *really* was spoken, not as you may have redesigned it or repeated it since. Be honest. Once you are clear, really *honestly clear,* about what transpired, take the incident apart in the following manner:

1. What did you expect of that person that they did not say or do? Write it down in your Journal. Go into detail. Elaborate. Write it all down. Use the word *should*.

   (*Should* is not a bad word, by the way. Looking carefully, you might notice that all upsets are based on *should*. The word simply implies a clash of value systems.) When you have this all down on paper, go on to step number 2.

2. Ask this question of yourself, being face-to-face honest: "What could I have said or done, that I did not, that would have let the other person know how I felt and what I wanted?" In other words, what, in hindsight, do you wish that you had said or done? Again, write it down. Every single word. Go inside and find it all. Give it written expression right now. Take your time. Be thorough. No one will see what you have written but you. *Be honest.*

As you complete the second part of this exercise, you might sense a creeping awareness that your **Resentment** comes not from what the other person did or said, but from what your expectations were of them and what you failed to communicate through either words or actions. Going even a step further, you might notice that there was an unspoken request on your part. Requests may be the most misidentified of verbal communications. We use phrases such as, "It sure would be nice if I could use your car tomorrow" or "I hate it when the music is so loud!" Comments such as those are statements of preference, not requests. The easiest way to know when you are making a request is to pave the way by beginning your comment with a simple phrase, such as "I have a request." For example, "My car is in the shop for the next three days and I have to be in the City tomorrow for an important meeting. I have a request. May I use your car?" or "That music is driving me crazy. I have a request. Please turn down the volume." Sound easy? Practice it once or twice to see how it feels.

If you have found this exercise enlightening, you will gradually realize that this awareness reduces upsets to very simple terms and dramatically shifts the accountability. If you have completed this exercise in earnest, you also may have begun to see that what upset you had nothing to do with the other person. Not a thing. It had to do with your expectations of them and how they let you down in some way. And there is a chasm of difference between *person* and *expectation of person*.

What causes us to shift into a negative, judgmental mode is our Should System—our expectation of how someone should be or what they should do. When we shift into a judgmental mode, we choose not to communicate clearly what we feel, nor do we ask for what we want. To justify our **Resentment**, we gossip about the offending incident with other people, defending our right to be hurt, resentful, and angry. Yet we never let the offender know what they did! Not knowing their offense, they repeat it, and we gloat and justify. We muck around in our own **Resentment**, yet we assume no responsibility for conveying our feelings, and frequently give excuses—"She never listens," "I might get fired," or "He's always so closed-minded." As if that weren't enough, we justify our silence and bloat our **Resentment** by reshaping the story each time we think about it or repeat it. Holy Memory kicks in making the story better with each telling, and digs the **Resentment** groove deeper and deeper. And all of this is about something that could have been cleared up *if we had spoken or acted*.

The previous two-part writing exercise can be literally transformational. The next time you are deeply upset, just pick up a pen and paper and write it just as you did a few moments ago.

This is a personal power exercise because it causes us to stand in the Truth, acknowledge what is really happening, and choose whether or not to take appropriate action. There is no room for excuses, gossip, self-justification, blame, or **Resentment**, only a clear choice on our part whether or not to act. And once we make that choice, just as when we make *any* choice, we have only two places inside in which to stand: in our mind, which is fearful, or in our heart, which knows only love. When we make any choice, we are standing in either one place or the other. Where we stand and how we choose is entirely up to us.

CHAPTER FOURTEEN

Creativity

It is a sin in the evolutionary process of God to try to suppress another's creative spirit.

· Paramhansa Yogananda ·

DECLARATION TO MY WHOLENESS

My creative spirit overflows

with my unique talents and abilities.

I F YOU ASK A ROOM full of thirty kindergarteners, "Who can draw?" thirty hands will shoot up excitedly. Young voices will eagerly compete to describe what they draw best. They may even frantically wave their paintings and shout, "See! Look what I drew!" Stand in front of the classroom of these same students once they are freshmen in high school and ask the same question. How many hands would be raised, even if hesitantly? Possibly two. On the outside, *maybe* three. It isn't that the creative ability no longer exists. What happens is that through the years we give creativity comparative standards, external value judgments, and a silent burial.

Early in life we begin to define **Creativity** by the norms the world has set in place. We *think* we're an artist, or a creative writer, or good with our hands until someone says, "You can't even color inside the lines!" or "You're a terrible speller!" or "What's *that* supposed to be?" We interpret these casual comments as the Gospel according to Grownups, and begin to disown our own unique creative abilities. We side with "them." In our young eyes "they" are wiser, older, and of course they love us and would not lie. Their casual opinion becomes Truth. We stop drawing or painting, we no longer express our innermost thoughts poetically or through writing little stories, and as far as clay modeling or woodworking go . . . well, we were never very good anyway. We start by saying, "Darn! I really loved my pictures so much!" or "It made me feel so happy when I was writing poetry," or "Shaping little bunnies out of clay made me feel so good inside," and then we end up saying, "Oh well, what do I know?" With our one last creative gasp we hesitantly affirm, "I wish I could, but I must be wrong. After all, 'they' know what creative is. And besides, no one mentioned feeling." With a deep sigh we begin to shovel earth on the grave of our unique creative self and bury it deep.

Any of this sound familiar? Well, I've got news for you. When you die, God isn't going to say, "Why weren't you more like da Vinci, Shakespeare, or Rodin?" God is going to look you straight in the eye and say, "I gave you everything you needed, and more. Why weren't you more like *you?*"

In *The American Heritage Dictionary,* the primary definition of the word *create* is "to cause to exist." **Creativity** is defined further as "characterized by originality and expressiveness." When we combine these two definitions, we have "One who causes something to exist that is characterized by originality and expressiveness."

Can you remember a time in your life in which you participated in a *creative instant?* I define a creative instant as an occurrence in which we tap into a Source much greater than ourselves and are able to express what we feel exquisitely, as though guided. It feels as though we have stepped into sacred territory and, for perhaps the first time, we are face to face with our own personal magnificence. If you've been there, you know exactly what I mean. If you aren't sure, then read on.

PRACTICE

Copy this paragraph in your Daily Journal.

When you are inspired by some great purpose, some extraordinary project, all your thoughts break their bonds; your mind transcends limitations, your consciousness expands in every direction, and you find yourself in a new, great and wonderful world. Dormant forces, faculties [and] talents become alive, and you discover yourself to be a greater person by far than you ever dreamed yourself to be.

Patanjali

Now put the paper down for a moment. Look at the appearance of your writing on the page. Is there a flowing motion, a sense of expressive freedom? Check out your Upper Zone. Is it tallish? By tallish I mean at least two- to two-and-a-half times the height of the Mid Zone.

#119 *faculties*

Or does it seem to be lopped off near the top of the Mid Zone rather than extended upward?

#120 *faculties*

If so, stretch your Upper Zone up-up-up to about two- to two-and-a-half times as tall as your Mid Zone. No shorter. No taller. Shorter and you are not willing to stretch; taller and you are denying your own worth and beginning to bluff.

One letter I want you to pay special attention to is the letter *f.* Go back over your writing to see what your *f*'s look like. There are many ways to write an *f,* but a few tendencies are revealing.

Are your *f*'s balanced? Something like this:

#121 *f f*

Please note that half of the letter appears above the baseline and half below. The *f* is the only trizonal lowercase letter in the Latin alphabet. As such, it encompasses our entire being: body, mind, spirit, and soul. Because of this, the *f* is the most sacred letter of the alphabet family. It leaves no zone untouched, and in it we cannot hide from our own creative, spiritual, loving, knowing Self. When a part of the letter is missing or minimally inscribed, however, we are avoiding giving attention to the part of us it reflects.

When I say "minimally inscribed" I am referring to missing parts or unemphasized zones. For example:

1. This *f* with retraces in both the Upper and Lower Zone, is proclaiming the nothing-for-me attitude. It reflects the person who is constantly doing for others, and as far as meeting their own needs, they aren't even in line. Underlying these retraces, however, is a person who desperately wants to be acknowledged, knows that they are special, but is unpracticed in expressing it.

2. Here we have the *daydreamer f*. An overactive Upper Zone allows room not only for ideas but for fantasy as well. But if you look at the Lower Zone, you will not see much activity there. This writer has a gigantic imagination, thinks and fantasizes, but does not manifest her or his dreams in day-to-day living.

3. This *f* is the opposite of the *daydreamer f*. No Upper Zone at all, only a forward-moving Lower Zone. This writer's projects are manifested through using someone else's ideas and plans, not their own. It doesn't mean they don't *have* them, it means that they are not using them.

4. This is the infamous self-sabotage *f*. Many handwriting books label this a fluidity stroke, but in my studies over many years, I have discovered an additional dimension to this letter.

By studying the motion of the loops, it becomes obvious that although the top loop is moving ahead, toward the future, the lower loop counters that action by regressing to the left, or the past. There is simply no forward movement here. It is one of the reasons this particular *f* is so valuable in reducing stress of all sorts. By drawing line after line of this letter, blood pressure goes down, breathing evens out, shoulders relax, and lines unfurrow on the brow. Why? Because it takes the forward-moving (or out of control) energy and puts on the brakes in a noninvasive manner, much like gently taking someone by the hand and quietly redirecting their course of action.

Among writers who are balanced in their approach to life, it represents those who will subtly sabotage themselves at the last moment, even though they may be bright and talented, or say that they want to be in committed relationships. Potential success or budding relationships will drop at their feet, unfulfilled. From studying the writing of reverse-*f*-lower-loopers, I have found evidence of two supporting attitudes: fear of success and fear of commitment.

The impact of the *f* is indeed overwhelming on one's life. It represents past, present, and future as well as body, mind, and spirit.

5. This is the balanced *f*. It represents the writer who is willing to use her or his abilities, talents, and gifts to serve humankind, with complete involvement, absolute trust in the "powers that be," and nonattachment to the results. Look at an *f* drawn this way as an archer's bow.

#123

It is comprised of three parts:

a) A fully-formed upper loop that houses one's personal, spiritual, and philosophical concepts as well as unique creativity and imagination.

b) A fully-formed lower loop facing to the right of the descender, which represents the writer's willingness to move into action.

c) A stroke that, as it completes the lower loop at the Mid Zone (everyday life), crosses back over the downstroke to the left creating a small tie loop (grabbing hold of all your resources), and shoots forward off to the right (future).

Imagine that the bow is Life, you are the arrow in the bow, and God is the archer. When you write the *archer's f* you are declaring, "I am an arrow in your bow, Lord. Use me!" When I find myself short on trust, I sit and write pages of these "*f*'s." If you want to experience the effects of this *f*, you might want to take a few moments and fill a page with them. They are powerful. They are inspirational.

To support the intentions inherent in this powerfully drawn *f*, be on the lookout for several counterproductive formations. Look again at the paragraph you copied and find any *d*'s. Do you make a loop in the stem? A loop in the *d* stem contains your sensitivity, your stuffed emotions, and, yes, your untapped creativity. If you find loops in your *d*'s any bigger than this

#124   *d*

they can sabotage your finest intentions. This barely perceptible loop indicates sensitivity to others and to oneself, but once it begins to grow beyond this size to this

you're involved in the oh-helpless-me syndrome and tend to take everything personally. You blame others for perceived wrongdoings, and you do not give yourself permission to speak what's in your heart if it will result in confrontation. Confront you won't, but gossip you will. You won't speak directly about an offense to the person with whom you're upset, but you will gossip *about* them behind their back and make them appear wrong while you, of course, justify your own position.

Fat *d* loops. Systemic poison to the soul's expression, and counter-productive to creativity in all areas of our lives. I call these loops

#128

Cleopatra loops because they graphically represent the "Queen of Denial." This type of person takes everyone else's burdens onto their own shoulders, yet when asked if they're doing all right (when they are not), or if they would like some help (when they really want and need it), always smiles sweetly and says, "Oh, I'm just fine, thanks. And thank you for the offer, but I can do this myself." These people do not give themselves permission to express what's really in their hearts on any level, especially when it comes to drawing a boundary or expressing their personal creativity. Nor are they practiced in asking for what they really want. Be immensely compassionate with this type of person, and know that what you say is being *interpreted* rather than *understood*. If there is even an outside chance of a misunderstanding, your comments will be mistranslated and taken personally. Before you go searching madly for samples of writing with *d* loops, check out your own writing for compassion strokes. (See Friendship, Forgiveness, and Honesty.)

Although the following loop resembles the Cleopatra loop, it has a distinct difference.

#129

This is called the *Santa Claus loop* because there is almost no circle (which reflects the ego self in the world), and the loop is leaning over the circle/self as though filled with the burdens of the world. I heard a one-line definition of a personality type that describes this writer to a *d*. This person is someone who, when they die, will have someone *else's* life flash before their eyes. Writers with this *d* may be immensely talented, but either deny it or don't have time for creativity because they are too concerned with other people's lives.

Overly sensitive, these writers are so busy taking on everyone else's burdens that they usually neglect their own needs. They may have the heart of a missionary, but do not take care of themselves, are often overweight or underweight because of poor eating habits, and almost always wear a smile. Their hypersensitive nature causes them to tuck their creativity away neatly, lest someone question their right to express it.

If you have large loops in your *d* stem consistently, this would be the ideal stroke for you to begin writing.

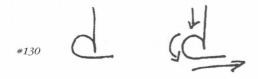

#130

This particular *d* is especially incisive for tapping into your own creativity and not worrying about what others may think. It is most effective in combination with the archer's *f* as a means of literally exploding your creative self. Notice the stroke pattern. It begins at the top of the stem, comes down to the baseline, creates a circle to the left, then finishes to the right, creating a subtle underscore beneath itself and reaffirming a self-reliant attitude. Do a few lines of them to see how it feels to you. If it feels odd or uncomfortable, it's working! Just keep repeating them until they begin to flow.

One final suggestion: Begin to underscore your signature each time you sign your name anywhere. For softness, use a curvy line rather than an angled one, and always end the stroke to the right. It will instill self-reliance without pushiness and you will soon set your own guidelines. You will not only be tapping into your creativity, you will begin living it!

Make your signature the same size as your handwriting. If you write very tiny, double the size of your writing! Life is too short to be invisible. Your signature makes a statement, declaring your image in the world. Underscore it modestly at first, then, as that feels comfortable, be brave. Here are a few examples.

#131

Design your own, one that suits who *you* say you are. If you're just tiptoeing into your creative self, have the underscore be the length of your signature, drawn softly and without angles. As that feels comfortable, it might be fun to continue the *paraph* (ending stroke) creatively beneath your name—softly.

#132

It is best not to encircle your signature. This symbolizes being wrapped up in yourself and needing protection from outside influences. Be careful, also, to write the ending stroke in a rightward direction. When any stroke ends to the left, the writer is looking to the past for approval, methods, and validation. The suggestion is to *under*score. Not to encircle. Not to draw a line through your name. (Don't cross yourself out!) Not to create an angular paraph that is analytical and critical. Simply to *under-*score!

By faithfully and methodically incorporating these changes, you will gradually unearth your own unique creative talents and begin to express them as *only you can*. You came into life with your own "specialness." No one has ever experienced or expressed life from your viewpoint, your exact set of experiences, or your unique flavor. And, for all time to come, no one ever will. Your gifts are uniquely yours and only yours. If you choose not to transform these gifts into creative action, they will die when you do, and they will never live in exactly the same way ever again. Only you can choose.

CHAPTER FIFTEEN

Wonder

Star light, star bright,

first star I see tonight,

I wish I may, I wish I might,

have the wish I wish tonight.

DECLARATION TO MY WHOLENESS

As a child of God I see the world as

flawless, pure, and safe.

WONDER IS NOT IN vogue these days. In fact, it never has been. You will have to search diligently to find books on the subject. **Wonder** is that quality we touch inside when we focus on the simple magnificence of a rainbow, marvel at a violinist teasing soul-stirring sounds by simply drawing a bow over four taut strings, or watch a spider spinning her web. When we stand back from any of these events and are deeply moved by the simple unbelievability of the creation, awestruck, we are experiencing **Wonder**.

A few months ago, my very short neighbor Jessica (age 2) grabbed my hand in hers and began pulling insistently. Through the ivy, across her driveway, and onto her front lawn we went. All the while she was squeezing my hand tightly, tugging me forward and shouting excitedly, "Wook! Wook! Wook, Vim!" I kept "wooking" in the direction her little finger was pointing, but all I saw were shrubs, flowers, and a pistachio tree. "What, Jessica? What is it you want me to see?" She let go of my hand, turned slightly,and pointed in a firm over-there motion with one final, "Wook, Vim, *wook!*" Then I saw it.

A spider web was anointing the distance between two shrubs, glistening with the fresh dew of early morning, catching the sunlight in such a way that it truly looked like a golden stained-glass window. "Oh, Jessica. I *see*. Thank you. Thank you." And I followed her example and sat on the damp grass and we just "wooked" together. **Wonder**.

Little Jess was not in awe from her mind; it was her heart that went pitter-patter when she caught sight of this miracle in action. She didn't anticipate the tensile strength of the web or estimate the time it took the spider to weave it. Nor did she, adultlike, think about what the threads were made of, or how many feet all these threads would measure if they were tied together, end to end. Nor did it occur to her innocent little mind to consider projecting mathematically how long it would take a human being, extrapolated out in proportion to the spider, to do the same thing.

I looked over at Jess, and a line from Sunday school crept up the corridors of my mind, and for the first time I really got it: "And unless ye shall be like little children . . ." I bowed to my mind with great respect, but I didn't invite it to our front yard party. I quietly slipped into my heart and just felt. **Wonder**. Sharing in the magnificence of the universe without having to understand.

PRACTICE

Copy this excerpt in your Daily Journal.

> *If I had influence with the good fairy who is supposed to preside over the christening of all children I should ask that her gift to each child in the world be a sense of wonder so indestructible that it would last throughout life, as an unfailing antidote against the boredom and disenchantments of later years, the sterile preoccupation with things that are artificial, the alienation from the sources of our strength. If a child is to keep alive his inborn sense of wonder without any such gift from the fairies, he needs the companionship of at least one adult who can share it, rediscovering with him the joy, excitement and mystery of the world we live in.*

Rachel Carson

Put your pen down and observe your writing. What does the baseline look like? Does it appear to shoot across the page as if driven from a bow? or does it have a gentle ever-so-slight softness? To magnetize **Wonder**, ease up on that baseline. Slow down your writing and hold the pen a little more lightly between your fingers. Breathe! Allow generous spacing between the letters; no compressed circle letters, please.

Is there a rigidity in the strokes or in the writing patterns?

#133 *excitement*

If so, you might want to loosen up. To do so you will have to slow down, but that's okay. We're here to experiment and have fun, not to win a race.

What about the connectives? Is there a dominance of angles?

#134 *mysteries*

Angles denote analytical thinking: the need to figure things out and to understand. There's nothing wrong with that, but it does squeeze the life out of **Wonder**. Not much room for seeing freshly when you are dealing with analysis and fixed thinking structures.

To draw out the open, receptive, childlike qualities that set the stage for **Wonder** within yourself, you might want to begin incorporating garlands now and again as connectives between letters.

#135 *mysteries*

Speaking of connectives, if you want to experience **Wonder** in your life continuously, do not connect each and every letter within a word. Use garlands when you do connect, and start breaking up words of five or more letters. This opens you up to the feeling and knowing self; the intuitive, sensitive child-self. Here is what I mean by breaking up words.

#136 *or din ary*

It is important to note here that I am referring to cursive writing and not to printing, which is an entirely separate phenomenon from writing.

Notice that I have left a visible space between the *r* and the *d* and between the *n* and the *a*. I did that on purpose. In fact, it's crucial to the following picking-up-the-pen exercise.

If your handwriting has most or all of your letters connected within words, begin disconnecting by writing the word *ordinary*. When you complete the *r*, STOP. Pick your pen up off the paper, leave a space between the *r* and the *d*, and begin the *d* at the *top of the circle*. Continue writing until you come to the *n* and end it in a downstroke to the baseline. Now pick up the pen again and begin the *a* at the top, just as you did with the *d*. Connect the letters *ary*. How did that feel? Do it once again. Slowly. Attentively. **o r d i n a r y**. Be aware of any resistance from your mind. If you have connected most of the letters in your words for many years, I promise you, you will have resistance.

Picture yourself being transported through life in a chauffeur-driven limousine. Your chauffeur's name is Logic & Predictability. This driver guides your thinking processes and helps you make decisions. By disconnecting letters now and again, you are delegating the chauffeur to the back seat and climbing into the front seat with a new and long-neglected friend, your own Inner Knowing. Not only are you renewing an old friendship, you have invited this welcome companion to drive for a while. Expect resistance! Remind yourself that the chauffeur has not been locked out of the car, but only a given a lesser role as a backseat driver. Invite input from Logic & Predictability in the decision-making process, but don't give in to its demands for having the final word.

Write this sentence in your Daily Journal, breaking up your words as you just did with the word *ordinary*.

Doodley dragons and quacky parrots always boisterously giggle at the antics of orange aardvarks dancing to a jazzy sonata in the moonlight.

Was that fun? Do it again!

By disconnecting the letters intermittently, as you did in this exercise, you are calling forth your intuitive, knowing self and giving it an elevated status. It will immediately begin to influence your decision-making in all areas of your life: mental, spiritual, emotional, and physical. Logic & Predictability will still be present, but in a lesser role. This writing change can help you slip out of your reasonable mind and unlatch the gate to your heart.

If you want immediate and direct access to your **Wonder**-full-Self heart feelings, when you use your Dialogue Book to create inner child right-hand/left-hand conversation, disconnect some of the letters within words using *both* hands. Practice this especially when you are super-sensitive or feeling helpless and vulnerable. Pick up your pen and see what happens. **Wonder** will guide you through the maze of your feelings right to the core of your soul. **Wonder** is as close as the tip of your pen.

CHAPTER SIXTEEN

Gratitude

Gratitude is a fruit of great civilization;

you do not find it among gross people.

· Dr. Samuel Johnson ·

DECLARATION TO MY WHOLENESS

All circumstances in my life

have been created just for me,

and I embrace them with a joyful heart.

G RATITUDE IS NOT JUST saying "thank you," nor is it merely being appreciative for what you have or who you are. Rather, it is the experience of stepping back and looking at all that you are and are not; all that you have and do not have; and all that you know and do not know. **Gratitude** is appreciating every circumstance that has been, and is now, in your life and embracing the entire package. Accompanying that grateful embrace are twinkling eyes, a smile that is pushed outward from an overflowing heart, and arms held wide in thanksgiving. **Gratitude** is twin sister to **Trust**. It is a state of heart that acknowledges all things as perfect, although not always understandable. It is feeling a sense of privilege at one's role as the ideal one to play in life.

Most of us consider ourselves to be grateful. Let's take a little straight-talking honesty quiz. Walk back in time into your life. Way back. Look at your family. Especially your parents. Take a breath, close your eyes, and really look. Go back to when you were very little—an infant, if you know stories about that time or can remember back that far. Are you grateful for every word your parents said or did not say and for everything they did or did not do? Close your eyes, pause, and reflect for a moment.

Now come forward through the years . . . to preschool, then elementary school. Are you grateful for what they gave to you and for what they withheld from you? For the loving support, overprotection, neglect, or abuse you experienced? Once again, close your eyes, reflect for a moment, and be present to those years. Now go on to high school, then college. Are you grateful for the understanding or lack of understanding they offered and for all that they were and were not? Close your eyes yet again and recall that time. Now bring your memories up to the present day, looking at who they are and who they are not. Are you grateful, or do you feel only anger, resentment, and blame? Hold on to the memories you have just brought forth as you read on.

Given who your parents were or are for you, and every situation that you have experienced because of your relationship with them, consider thoughtfully the following questions:

- If your parents had said or done anything differently, would you be the same person you are today?

- If you had not endured each and every experience, would you be the same caring, introspective person you are? Would you have the same depth of understanding?

- Would you be reading this book?

- Would you even be curious about personal transformation?

- Would you be aware of, or searching for, the fulfillment of a rich inner life?

- Would you understand that the only way life changes is when we change?

- Or would you be pointing like a spoiled child to everyone and everything else insisting that *they* change to make you happy?

Just tuck all that in your heart for reference.

Here are a few more heart-tuckers. What about the condition known as *suffering*, a term most often used when someone or something we treasure is taken away or leaves our life? Is **Gratitude** possible then? Or are anger, hurt, and bitterness the only alternatives? Life's important lessons push us out of our comfort zone and invite us to reach beyond the walls of our petty ways of thinking. We are given unparalleled opportunities to expand our view of life and, ultimately, to transform it. Finely honed, those lessons carve away what does not nurture our highest good. They are an invitation to stand back, review who we are, then choose whether to complain, blame, and suffer, or, with a joyful heart, to embrace our life's path as the perfect one for us. We have absolute freedom to accept or to decline the invitation. **Gratitude** is embracing life's lessons without needing to understand.

PRACTICE

Copy this excerpt in your Daily Journal.

Gratitude comes from the root word gratus, which means pleasing. The obvious interpretation is that when you are pleased with something, you are grateful. A second interpretation—the more radical one, and therefore the one we prefer—is that when you are grateful, then you are pleased, not by the thing, but by the gratitude. In other words, in order to feel pleased, be grateful.... Appreciate the things that are so magnificent, you took them for granted decades ago. What are we talking about? Your senses. Quick! Name all five!... Then there's the brain, and the body, and the emotions, and walking, talking, thumbs. Thumbs? Sure: Try to pick up some things without using your thumbs.

The attitude of gratitude: the greatful feeling.

John-Roger and Peter McWilliams

Look at the appearance of your writing. Not at "neat" or "sloppy," but at the flowing looseness about it. Is there a tight constrictedness in the letters or spacing? If it is tight and measured as opposed to loose and easy, you might want to loosen your grip on the pen a bit and let the writing flow more easily. Slow down. Breathe. Leave consistent breaks in your words. (See #136.) This will allow you to think more with your heart than with your mind and open you to interpreting your past experiences with a lack of rigidity and blame. A certain softness and acceptance will occur. Begin to incorporate extended final strokes at the ends of words (but not as the final stroke at the end of a line).

#137 *The great full feeling*

Don't let them go in an upward direction, just outward as though they were reaching out to invite the next word to play. This will feed your generosity of spirit by encouraging you to reach out to others.

Keep the *e, l,* and *h* loops open, and your heart will follow suit.

#138 *Joyful heart*

Gratitude: Seeing all of Life as a gift, then removing the wrapping paper.

One Final Paraph . . .

Each time you begin to write, imagine that the sheet of paper before you is your life. With each movement of the pen, be aware that you, the author, are reaffirming the attitudes with which you shape it. No one else is responsible for the plot and character development. By moving the pen consciously, you reaffirm positive, uplifting, joy-stirring qualities. Your past history and other people no longer determine your decisions, and you become the conscious author of your life. Gently begin to remove the qualities that are no longer appropriate for who you say you are, and introduce those that support your highest intentions.

Used daily, applied graphotherapy can be a powerful tool in the process of self-actualization. It does not bypass the process of dealing honestly with the issues you have, it simply shortens it. *Knowing* about this marvelous science will make very little difference in your life. *Using* it will not only create miracles, it can redirect the course of your life.

I have thousands of clients who can attest to the power of altering handwriting strokes as a means of reshaping their lives. If you are a skeptic, give it a chance. You have nothing at all to lose—and who knows, you might even learn something about yourself.

By using your Daily Journal and Dialogue Book every day, you can make a dramatic difference in the way you approach life and how life, in turn, responds to you. You will become acutely aware that life is no great puzzle to be mastered; it is simply a mirror. You may notice, too, that as you change, your environment responds to the new you. People start treating you differently. Life eases off. It begins to work the way you want it to.

If you are stalled, feel blocked, or are puzzled as to why you keep repeating a particular pattern in your life, do your handwriting practice every day without fail. Follow the directions explicitly for three weeks— just three weeks—and see what changes occur. Above all, keep that Log of Miracles! It will be written proof that you are making a difference in your own life.

BIBLIOGRAPHY

BIBLIOGRAPHY

Dr. Samuel Johnson and James Boswell. *Journey to the Western Isles of Scotland*. Editor, Allan Wendt. 1965.

Rachel Carson. *The Sense of Wonder*. Harper & Row. 1945.

Course in Miracles. Foundation for Inner Peace. 1985.

Stephen R. Covey. *The 7 Habits of Highly Effective People*. Simon & Schuster, 1989.

Ram Dass. *Be Here Now*. The Lama Foundation. 1972.

Teilhard De Chardin. *Building the Earth*. Dimension Books. 1979.

Ralph Waldo Emerson. Notable American Author Series. Reprint of *Poems,* 1847.

Ruth Gendler. *The Book of Qualities*. Turquoise Mountain Publications. 1984.

James Hilton, *Time & Time Again*. Little, Brown. 1953.

Benjamin Hoff. *The Tao of Pooh*. Dutton. 1982.

Maxwell Maltz, M.D. *Psycho-Cybernetics*. Prentice Hall, Inc. 1960.

John-Roger and Peter McWilliams. *Life 101*. Bantam Books. 1991.

Thomas Merton. *New Seeds of Contemplation*. New Directions. 1972.

Thomas Merton. *New Seeds of Contemplation*. New Directions. 1972.

Peggy Tabor Millan. *Mary's Way*. Celestial Arts. 1991.

Patanjali. *The Yoga Sutras of Patanjali*. Susil Gupta (India). 1955.

Norman Vincent Peale. *Enthusiasm Makes the Difference*. Prentice Hall, Inc. 1965.

Ramtha. *Ramtha*. Sovereignty, Inc. 1986.

SARK. *A Creative Companion*. Celestial Arts. 1991.

Dr. Robert H. Schuller. *Tough Times Never Last, But Tough People Do!* Bantam Books. 1984.

From the poem "Practicing Forgiveness" in the book *Accept this Gift*. Edited by Frances Vaughn, Ph.D., and Roger Walsh, M.D., Ph.D. Jeremy P. Tarcher, Inc. 1983.

Terry Cole-Whitaker. *What You Think of Me is None of My Business*. Oak Tree Publications. 1979.

John Wooden. *They Call Me Coach*. Contemporary Books. 1988.

Paramhansa Yogananda. From a talk given in Hollywood, CA. 1937. © Self-Realization Fellowship.

Paramhansa Yogananda. *Man's Eternal Quest*. © Self Realization Fellowship. 1982.

GLOSSARY

GLOSSARY

Angle Any written formation that has two lines intersecting at the baseline. Written repeatedly, this trait indicates a writer who analyzes easily and automatically.

Arcade This stroke resembles an archway. It symbolizes a protective nature. A person with consistent arcades often approaches problems in a methodical, step-by-step fashion and is slow to take risks.

Archer's *f* There are four parts to this letter, each of which is an essential element of the archer's *f*. 1) The beginning stroke is at the baseline and reaches into the Upper Zone, creating a loop. 2) This stroke descends into the Lower Zone, creating a loop to the right of the descender. The height and width of this loop is in balance with the upper loop. 3) As it comes back up to complete the lower loop, it crosses back over the descender, creating a small tie loop. 4) As soon as the tie is drawn, the finishing stroke drives off to the right.

Backlash stroke This is an ending stroke that reaches up and back over the word, ending in a leftward direction. It indicates blame of self and others, stemming from the past.

Backslant This handwriting leans to the left. Slow to trust, these writers have chosen to withhold who they are and what they really feel. This trait stems from a childhood that the writer perceived as unsafe. Hundreds of left-handers through the years have explained to me again and again, "I write with a backslant because I'm left-handed." I just didn't believe it, so in the early 70s I began a three-year research project to see if, in fact, this could be true. Of the 3,400 samples I studied, my findings indicated that eight times as many right-handers wrote with a backslant than left-handers.

Baseline This is the imaginary line we create for our letters to sit upon as we write.

Bowl stroke This stroke occurs in a *t* crossbar that connects itself to the following letter. It dips down, creating a deep bowl-like shape before it reaches out to the next letter. It represents a lack of direction and few, if any, goals being acted upon by the writer.

Communication letters: *a o d g q p.*

So called because they reflect our communication skills in all areas of life. Each of the communication letters is simply the letter *a* (ego self) active in different parts of our lives.

- The letter *a* reflects the degree of comfort we have with our physical appearance and our ability to interact confidently.

- The letter *o* is simply the *a* with a different focus. It reflects our verbal communication skills.

- The letter *d* is, once again, the *a* (our ego self in the world), but after it encircles the self, it begins to reach into the Upper Zone. As it journeys upward it is asking the question, "Who approves of me or of what I am doing?" Think of it as a periscope. The higher it goes, the more the writer is searching for approval. The average *d* stem is two to two and a half times as tall as the Mid Zone. The short, retraced *d* stem reflects the independent thinker who cannot be shamed or cajoled into conforming to anything that would conflict with his value system. A looped *d* stem reflects a person who finds it difficult to speak their truth in a straightforward manner. In handwriting, a loop is always a container. The *d* loop is filled with hurt feelings and perceived injustices. The larger the loop, the more it contains; the more it contains, the deeper the hurt.

- The letter *g* has to do with personal relationships, going, as it does, into the Lower Zone. It also reflects sexual energy, the need for movement and activity, and the degree of independence or interdependence we exhibit in our daily lives.

- The letter *q* is the letter of altruism. It reflects how readily the writer contributes to others without expecting anything in return.

- The letter *p* reflects our sense of personal lovability and the need to defend it or to be at peace with who we are, as we are.

Compressed writing

This writing appears to be squeezed from the sides, much like an accordion. It indicates a person who often talks a great deal, usually on self-centered topics, and rarely listens. Their perception of other persons' realities is severely restricted.

Control stroke Indicated by a linear stroke that goes in a direction from upper left to lower right. This can be in a *t* cross-bar, an *i* dot, or printed capital letters such as *E* or *F*. This stroke reflects a writer who needs to be in control. If it is consistently repeated, this control extends into all areas of the writer's life.

Cleopatra loop This is an extraordinarily large, full loop that occurs in the *d* stem. Cleopatra writers stuff all their feelings and do not confront those with whom they are upset, yet talk behind their backs as a means of justifying how they feel. They smile a lot. When you see that this writer needs help, and you volunteer help, you will be greeted with a comment that goes something like this: "Thanks a lot. I really don't need any help. I can handle this myself, but I appreciate the offer." Yet they truly want to learn how to reach out. More than that, they want to know how to receive. I call it a Cleopatra loop because she was the "Queen of Denial."

Crossbar This is the horizontal bar that creates the letter *t* by intersecting the stem. It represents the writer's will-power.

Daydreamer *f* This particular letter *f* has an extraordinarily large upper loop and no lower loop.

Delta *d* This letter *d* is formed by making the circle, then reaching up into the Upper Zone, creating a single arching stroke that usually ends to the left. At times it will have a finishing angle to the right. It is called the delta *d* because it resembles the Greek letter delta.

This writer often is fascinated with any discipline that has roots (history and genealogy are good examples) and may have literary tendencies.

Descender This is a stroke that dives into the Lower Zone.

Detrose loop Detrose means "in a rightward direction." This loop is small, tight, and drawn in a rightward direction. In both the Palmer and Zaner-Bloser systems it introduces thirteen capital letters. Loops, regardless of their size or location, are always containers. Where they occur tells what they contain. A detrose loop contains suspicion, envy, jealousy, and an attitude of egocentrism. It lives in fear and severely restricts generosity and gratitude.

Downstroke This is a stroke that is written in a vertical, downward direction. It can occur in any of the three zones.

Figure-eight *g* This letter *g* is written so it resembles the numeral eight. The letter begins at the top of the Mid Zone, describing a softly drawn half circle open to the right, and the descender begins a soft and generous loop formation; the ascender completes the motion and ends at the baseline, off to the right. This is one of the most powerful strokes you can use to feed the soul; it opens up your heart and lets the creative juices flow.

Garland This stroke is just the opposite of the arcade. It reflects an open hand: the ability both to give and to receive. It symbolizes one who is a people person, whose nature is to reach out to others. Garlands can occur in letter formations as well as in connective strokes between letters.

Handwriting systems.

These are the three most frequently used handwriting systems in the United States.

- **Palmer System**

Aa Bb Cc Dd
Ee Ff Gg Hh
Ii Jj Kk Ll
Mm Nn Oo Pp
Qq Rr Ss Tt
Uu Vv Ww
Xx Yy Zz .. ?
$1\,2\,3\,4\,5\,6\,7\,8\,9\,10$

• Zaner-Bloser System

- **D'Nealian System**

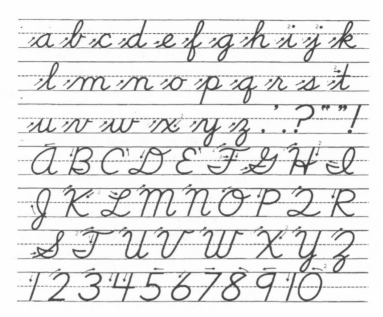

There are countless negative strokes in each of these handwriting systems, but since this book is not designed as a text, I will mention only the three most destructive so that you can eliminate them from your handwriting.

- The first is the retraced downstroke in the Mid Zone. This stroke is exceedingly repressive because it squelches the expression of the creative mind and reinforces fear and conformity rather than honesty and creativity. It encourages an imitative attitude and directs the writer to duplicate the world around him and follow other people's dreams. It reinforces lockstep obedience.

- Another red flag is the placement of the *t* crossbar. In all of these handwriting systems the writer is directed to cross *t*'s at the top of the Mid Zone. In handwriting, the *t* crossbar is the willpower stroke. Its placement reinforces the writer's self-image, self-esteem, and belief in her- or himself to be able to achieve. If crossed at the top of the Mid Zone, it will keep superior achievements and a solid sense of self-esteem in check.

- The third nefarious and powerfully negative stroke is the detrose loop. It puts a damper on the creative mind and stifles the spirit.

Here is the **Vimala System of Handwriting**. Now you can see what a positive and self-affirming alphabet looks like. Each stroke reaffirms creativity, aliveness, and a sense of personal worth. Note the differences between this alphabet and the traditional ones. If you want to experience the attitudes that accompany the letter formations, simply write all three of them as they are here and see how you feel inside as you move the pen.

The Vimala Alphabet

A B C D E F G H I J J K
L L M M N N O P Q R S
T U U V W W X Y Z Z Z & &
a b c d e e f g g h i j k l l m n
o o p q r r r s t t u v w x y z z
st th sh 1 2 3 4 5 6 7 8 9 0 ? !

Ligature A ligature is a letter, part of which creates the one that follows. Next to the ampersand (which is an artistic form of *et*), the *th* is the most commonly used ligature today. The *th* ligature represents a fluid thinker who has a flexible attitude and copes well in stressful situations. See *bowl stroke*.

Loops Loops appear in all zones. They are always containers. Where they occur determines what they contain. A loop in any zone can reinforce either positive or negative attributes. It depends entirely upon how it is drawn.

Margins A margin is the space we leave around the outer edges of our writing. It defines the area we have chosen to occupy in life and delineates the boundaries we have set.

Miles of lace Graceful and quieting, this gently flowing stroke resembles vertical layers of written capital *L*'s connected to one another. Drawing them repeatedly reduces tension and lowers blood pressure. Great used as a doodle when you are encountering stressful situations.

Paraph The final stroke of a signature.

Printing There are three kinds of printing, each distinct from the other.

- Upper/lower case printing. This is an individual variation that resembles what we learned in elementary school. A person who consistently prints has a way of keeping people at a discreet distance—not like a wall, more like a wire fence.

- Block printing. Every character in block printing is a capital letter. It is often angular in appearance. Blocks are for building walls. Writers whose mode of written communication is *always* block printing have put a wall around their heart and often are on the defensive. Every block printer I have ever worked with has suffered a deep trauma at some time in life and has not found a safe environment in which to express it and to heal.

- Printscript. This type of writing is a combination of writing and printing, distinguished by the following characteristics: some letters are connected while others are not, the letters are exceedingly basic in appearance, and there are few, if any, loops or introductory stroke patterns.

Propeller strokes These strokes are formed by creating a tall, soft, and slender loop in the Upper Zone, having the stroke then dive downward into the Lower Zone to create a matching loop that is on the *left* of the downstroke. The final stroke ends at the baseline and is used to create the next propeller. Excellent for reducing stress and fatigue. Do not ever use this stroke as a substitute for the letter *f,* as it is a contraindicator for a smooth, forward motion. Its purpose is to slow things down and to reverse the flow of energy.

Pull-away stroke This is an upstroke that pulls away from the downstroke at the baseline, creating a V shape. It occurs most frequently in the lowercase *m, n, h, k,* and the printscripted *r.* This stroke is exceedingly powerful for creating velocity in one's life. It is a dynamic alternative to the retraced downstroke, and is designed for the writer who wants to create and develop a unique vision of how the world could be. It supports risk-taking and adventure, and encourages the explosion of potential into action. Written faithfully, consistently, and with purpose, this stroke can incite a creative riot in your life.

Reining-in stroke This stroke is named for its movement. It prevents the creative energy from continuing in a forward motion and reins it in. Extremely repressive, the writer of this stroke is kicking the horse and pulling in on the reins at the same time. It occurs most often in the *m, n, h,* and *r.*

Reining-out stroke This stroke releases the constrictive movement of the reining-in stroke by releasing the tight movement and allowing it to move freely in a rightward direction.

Retraced downstroke in the Mid Zone.

This stroke occurs in traditional writing systems in the letters *m, n, h,* and *k.* It first goes down to the baseline, then as the pen moves upward from the baseline, it retraces the stroke that just went down. It is a Class Number One Fear Stroke. If you feel you have something worthwhile to contribute to humanity, do not ever use this stroke. Above all, do not teach it to children—unless, of course, they are in special training to be robots.

Santa Claus loop This loop occurs in the letter *d.* The initial circle is exceedingly small, if visible at all, and the loop in the stem is wide, full, and leans heavily over the weakly drawn circle (ego self). It is called the Santa Claus loop because this writer's supersensitive nature causes him to take on responsibility for the problems of the whole world (at the expense of his own), stuff them, then carry them through life like a weighty, overstuffed pack on his back.

Self-sabotage stroke.

This seductive stroke is created by writing the letter *f* with a reversed lower loop. It is also called the propeller stroke because it looks like one. Because forward-moving energy is retarded by creating a lower loop of this nature, one who writes this stroke with consistency has great difficulty with commitment and completion.

Spacing Spacing refers to the distance between letters in a word (the space we allow for personal expression); the distance between letters in a line of writing (the space we leave for others); and the distance between lines (the space we create in the world for ourselves).

Springboard stroke

This is a rigid, inflexible stroke that starts from beneath the baseline and drives into the Mid or Upper Zone with firm purpose. It indicates resentment.

Stem The vertical stroke in the letters *d* and *t*.

Stroke endings • Blunt. Blunt endings reflect a decisive thinker. (Felt-tip pens don't count). Blunt endings to the baseline reflect a decisive person with a positive attitude.

• Feathered. Feathered endings reflect a person who has a difficult time making up his mind. When they appear on the right of the *t* crossbar they reflect a person who can be sarcastic.

Umbrella *t* This powerful stroke is the crossbar on the letter *t* drawn with a slight bow shape, resembling an umbrella. This stroke reinforces self-discipline and the ability to say No! to old habits you want to be rid of.

Wedge Any written formation that has two intersecting lines that form a tent shape, like an inverted letter V.

Willpower stroke Willpower is represented by the *t* crossbar. It declares the nature of ones personal belief in oneself, goal-setting, self-image, self-esteem, and the willingness, or lack thereof, to stretch and strive. This stroke has many facets: its height on the stem, the pressure with which it is drawn, how it is balanced on the stem, the direction in which it goes, and the nature of how it begins and how it ends.

Zones There are three zones in handwriting: the Upper Zone, the Mid Zone, and the Lower Zone.

- The Upper Zone represents the mind. It stores philosophical or spiritual concepts and unique creative ideas.

- The Mid Zone represents day-to-day life, the mundane part of living. Look at the borders defining the Mid Zone as railroad tracks. It is in this area that we tend to our day-to-day activities—right here, right now.

- The Lower Zone represents our attitude toward relationships and our own sexuality. It also indicates our need for movement and change and the degree to which we prefer to be project oriented. It also tells whether we prefer many friends, only a few, or solitude.